At Issue

Are Cults a
Serious Threat?

Other Books in the At Issue Series:

At Issue

Are Cults a
Serious Threat?

Katherine Swarts, Book Editor

GREENHAVEN PRESS

An imprint of Thomson Gale, a part of The Thomson Corporation

Detroit • New York • San Francisco • New Haven, Conn. • Waterville, Maine • London

Christine Nasso, *Publisher*
Elizabeth Des Chenes, *Managing Editor*

LIBRARY OF CONGRESS CATALOGING-IN-PUBLICATION DATA

Are cults a serious threat? / Katherine Swarts, book editor.
    p. cm. -- (At issue)
Includes bibliographical references and index.
ISBN-13: 978-0-7377-2358-8 (lib. : alk. paper)
ISBN-10: 0-7377-2358-0 (lib. : alk. paper)
ISBN-13: 978-0-7377-2359-5 (pbk. : alk. paper)
ISBN-10: 0-7377-2359-9 (pbk. : alk. paper)
 1. Cults. I. Swarts, Katherine.
 BP603.Z74 2006
 209--dc22

                                                    2006022974

Printed in the United States of America
10 9 8 7 6 5 4 3 2 1

Contents

Introduction

Since the 1970s, horrifying or baffling incidents of violence involving little-known and radical religious groups called cults have generated headlines and public alarm; today, the image of a cult can still make mainstream society shudder. The word alone evokes memories of the 1978 Jonestown tragedy, in which over six hundred followers of the charismatic leader Jim Jones poisoned themselves to escape what they saw as outside persecution; of the 1993 burning of the Branch Davidian compound in Waco, Texas (eighty-two fatalities); of the 1995 Aum Shinrikyo sarin gas attack in Tokyo (twelve fatalities); and of the 1997 Heaven's Gate ritual suicide in California (thirty-nine fatalities). In the early years of the twenty-first century, terrorist groups (not "cults" in the strictest religious sense, but examples of organized, religiously motivated, us-against-the-world fanaticism) are a serious concern. And less a threat to public security, but nonetheless heartrending for those affected, are groups whose members renounce all connections with the "corrupt world" —including their own families.

Unfortunately, the stigma of such notorious incidents also causes a "guilt by association" problem for more benign religious groups who are labeled cults for their unorthodox theologies or practices. As journalist Melissa Evans reported in the *Oakland Tribune* in November 2003, "99.9 percent of [such groups] do not pose danger." Most objective observers today give such groups the more neutral name "new religious movements," a term scholars have adopted to avoid the sinister connotations often associated with the word *cult*.

What makes a group a cult (as opposed to a religion, a denomination, or a movement) is the subject of endless debate. Various broad definitions of the word located through any Internet search are benign enough: "the totality of *external* religious practice and observance"; "a system or community of religious worship and ritual"; "the formal means of expressing religious reverence." According to such definitions a cult is, technically, the sum of practices and culture in *any* religion.

More often, however, a cult is perceived as a dangerously unorthodox, if not sinister, group—at best a "bunch of loonies" who chant strange words and wear strange clothes; at worst a group that lures innocent students to "retreats" where they are turned into brainwashed zombies, or the followers of a mad guru who expects unquestioning obedience, grows rich on property confiscated from followers and profits generated by shady ventures, and inspires criminal acts. There is little disagreement that such radical, overtly destructive groups pose a legitimate threat.

Confusion arises when the label is applied not only to such groups but to minority sects that were once as new, or as small, as emerging religious sects today. Is Mormonism, founded in the early nineteenth century and today reporting millions of members who fit reasonably well into society, a cult? Many orthodox Christians say yes, because Mormonism claims to be Christian although its theology is incompatible with traditional Christianity. "The problem with Mormonism is that it contradicts, modifies, and expands on the Bible," reports the Christian online network Got Questions.org, founded by Calvary Theological Seminary (Kansas City) graduate S. Michael Houdmann. "Mormons . . . are involved in a false religion that distorts the nature of God."

Is Messianic Judaism, which combines Jewish and Christian theology, a cult? Many Jews say yes. "If we look at the definition of a destructive cult as set forth in virtually every study of cultism [deceptive recruitment, submission to leadership, hostility to the outside world]," says countercult organization Jews for Judaism (directed by rabbi/lecturer Bentzion Kravitz of Los Angeles) "it becomes clear that these groups fit the bill. [Their] missionary groups . . . are active worldwide."

Merely seeking converts—especially from other religions—can in itself draw the "cult" label in a society of cultural diversity and open-mindedness.

Simply being a religious minority can invite the label "cult," with political consequences. For example, the French government attracted international attention in the early 2000s by passing laws that referred to "mental manipulation" and restricted the activity of "sects," including some Christian groups. Whether or not, as some charged, the government's actual motive was to restrict the foreign influence associated with such movements, labeling a religion a "cult" *is* often a power play—a way to protect the status quo, or simply discredit an opponent.

Finally, many practices associated with destructive cults have counterparts in the major religions. Nearly all religions (at least in pure traditional form) consider their scriptures divinely inspired, and their theology the best way, if not the only way, of understanding life. "Christians reject religious pluralism in the sense that more than one religion can be said to have the truth," freely admit Anton and Janet Hein-Hudson of the Christian Web site Apologetics Index. "Cult apologists label this exclusivism as 'intolerance' or 'bigotry.'" Certainly many harmless, law-abiding adherents of the major world religions take their faith seriously enough to seek converts or strive to avoid "worldly influences." And many mainstream congregations have official or unofficial lists of what is "sinful" and look with disfavor on any member who disagrees. Mainstream denominations may engage in high-pressure evangelistic meetings, with a hellfire-and-brimstone approach an outsider could be excused for taking as indoctrination or brainwashing. And students of history learn that in other historical eras, "real" religions have become threats in their own right—consider the bloody battles of the Crusades or the terror tactics of the Inquisition against religious heretics.

Therein lies the central issue in deciding whether cults are a serious threat: ensuring freedom of religion for minorities while protecting society (and recruits) from the few truly dangerous groups—groups that often, ironically, spring from more orthodox religions. The contributors to *At Issue: Are Cults a Serious Threat?* debate this and other aspects of religious cults.

Cults Are Prone to Crime and Violence

Robert L. Snow

Robert L. Snow is an Indianapolis police captain and commander of the department's homicide branch, with over thirty years of police experience. He is the author of Deadly Cults: The Crimes of True Believers, The Militia Threat, *and* Murder 101.

In 1995 the Japanese cult Aum Shinrikyo, recognized as a legitimate religion since 1989, released poisonous nerve gas in the Tokyo subways. Twelve people died and over five thousand were injured. Subsequent investigation proved that the cult, which believed in imminent worldwide apocalypse, was guilty of many other crimes, including at least two dozen murders and over half a dozen kidnappings. Aum Shinrikyo is but one example of the violent inclinations of cults and of the crimes they commit against both outsiders and their own members. Dozens of cults have murdered defectors and opponents, abducted new recruits, and physically or sexually abused their members. The unpleasant effects can long outlast cult membership; many former cultists suffer from "post-cult trauma syndrome," characterized by depression, lack of mental and emotional control, and a sense of isolation.

By a little after 8:00 A.M. on March 20, 1995, five containers of the extremely lethal nerve gas sarin, a chemical so lethal a single drop on the skin can kill, had been set up at five

Robert L. Snow, *Deadly Cults: The Crimes of True Believers*. Westport, CT: Praeger Publishers, 2003, pp. 15–27. Copyright © 2003 by Robert Snow. All rights reserved. Reproduced by permission of Greenwood Publishing Group, Inc., Westport, CT.

different locations within the Tokyo subway system. Suddenly, according to news reports from all over the world, as the unaware subway passengers boarded the cars or stood waiting for their trains, the containers began spewing deadly fumes. Before the Tokyo subway system, which handles over five million passengers a day, could be evacuated and the nerve gas neutralized, 12 people died and more than 5,500 needed medical attention, with at least 75 of these listed in critical condition. Tokyo citizens were outraged and flabbergasted, not only by such a cruel terrorist attack in a country that had mostly avoided such incidents in the past but even more so because the authorities eventually discovered that the attack had been carried out by members of what most citizens had viewed as a peaceful, religious group: Aum Shinrikyo (the true teaching of Aum).

"I thought Japan was a safe country," said a subway passenger after the attack. "It's really awful for us to see this kind of incident take place."

In late March 1995, the police raided the headquarters of Aum Shinrikyo in the village of Kamikuishiki, about 70 miles southwest of Tokyo. There they discovered a complex full of secret passages and hidden rooms. They also found a secret laboratory, where the deadly nerve gas had been produced. However, along with the evidence of nerve gas production, the police additionally confiscated $7.9 million in cash and 22 pounds of gold. While searching the complex, the police also discovered more than 50 people in advanced stages of malnutrition who were wandering the complex aimlessly, and they freed 7 people who claimed that they had been held prisoner by the cult. Some weeks later, the police arrested the leader of the Aum Shinrikyo cult, a nearly blind former herbalist named Shoko Asahara, who had been forecasting a message of impending global doom for several years.

The 12 dead and 5,500 injured in the Tokyo subway attack, however, weren't the only victims of the Aum Shinrikyo cult. Police suspect that, before the subway attack, the cult had murdered at least two dozen other people. According to authorities, to get rid of the bodies of these victims, the cult used an industrial-sized microwave oven that could reduce bodies to dust and a cement-grinding machine that could pulverize bodies.

How did this all begin? How did a religious cult become involved in mass murder?

Following recognition by the Japanese government as a religion, the Aum Shinrikyo cult quickly began gathering both recruits and generous donations.

The Growth of a Murderous Cult

In 1989, Asahara, who claimed to have obtained enlightenment while on a trip to India, and who, before becoming a guru, had made his living as an herbalist, received notice from the Japanese government that Aum Shinrikyo had been officially recognized as a religion in Japan. This official recognition means that a group can operate without any government oversight or interference. Several years before, Asahara had attained a bit of fame as a religious figure when a Japanese occult magazine, *Twilight Zone*, published a photograph that claimed to show him levitating.

In the early 1990s, following recognition by the Japanese government as a religion, the Aum Shinrikyo cult quickly began gathering both recruits and generous donations. Soon communes run by Aum Shinrikyo began appearing all over Japan and quickly began filling up with young recruits. Aum Shinrikyo members, wearing white robes and standing on street corners and at subway entrances, would hand out invitations to free yoga classes. Those accepting the invitation, and who appeared to be good candidates for recruitment, were then shown videotapes of Asahara seemingly levitating, flying, and passing through walls. The recruits were promised that they too, with the proper training, could accomplish similar feats.

Interestingly, along with recruiting many of Japan's disaffected youth, the cult also attracted a number of highly educated individuals, including physicians, attorneys, chemists, and other scientists, among them even a virus and genetics researcher. It was through recruiting and indoctrinating these types of individuals, and then using their talents, that the cult managed to successfully manufacture and dispense the deadly nerve gas. By 1995, what had started out as a small religious group a decade before had grown to comprise more than 50,000 followers and reportedly more than $1 billion in assets.

However, since much of these assets had come from converts who turned over everything they owned to the cult, and who were also encouraged to give the cult other family property, family members of these cult converts naturally became concerned. They soon founded an organization called Parents of Aum Children. However, the cult didn't appreciate this type of organized opposition. An attorney who worked for the Parents of Aum Children, after a confrontation with Aum Shinrikyo officials, mysteriously disappeared, as did his wife and small child. An Aum Shinrikyo member later reportedly confessed to the police that an Aum Shinrikyo hit squad had entered the attorney's apartment, killed the three family members, and then buried their bodies, which the police later recovered.

From Philosophy to Politics to Violence

During the early years of the cult, Asahara expounded its philosophy of Buddhism, which at first stated that followers must find the middle ground between excessive self-indulgence and harsh self-deprivation. Like most cult leaders, however, Asahara later exempted himself from any of these requirements. While the Aum Shinrikyo cult eventually required members to take a vow of chastity and adhere to strict dietary requirements, Asahara lived with his wife and indulged in fine food and other luxuries. In addition to setting down strict rules and requirements for cult members, the Aum Shinrikyo cult also created a special "action squad," headed by a former Japanese underworld figure who had joined the cult. This squad's purpose was to kidnap and bring back any cult members who tried to leave the group.

In 1990, before forming his action squad and before coming under police suspicion, Asahara and 24 Aum Shinrikyo members ran for election to Japan's parliament. They were soundly defeated. This greatly disturbed Asahara, who had always seen himself as a new Buddha who would be proclaimed by the world as its savior. This rejection by Japanese voters, many feel, is what shifted Asahara's thinking to that of a global doomsday prophet. In a speech given on the cult's radio program just days before the Tokyo subway attack, Asahara reportedly told the audience, "Wake up my disciples! With no regrets, with full courage, let's go to our death!"

The Aum Shinrikyo cult isn't the only cult to have demonstrated a propensity for deadly violence.

In 1992, in a self-published book, *Declaring Myself the Christ*, Asahara professed that in addition to his belief in Buddhism, he believed himself to be the reincarnation of Jesus Christ. He also began making his prophecies for armageddon [the end of the world] which he forecast would begin in July 1999. Although most of humanity would perish in the end times, Asahara said that a small pocket of humanity, consisting of Aum Shinrikyo members, would survive to rebuild civilization. . . .

Other Violent Cults

The Aum Shinrikyo cult isn't the only cult to have demonstrated a propensity for deadly violence. "The biggest terrorist threat is no longer from traditional terrorists, but from religious sects," says Bruce Hoffman of the [US-based] Center for Terrorism. "[Palestinian terrorist] Abu Nidal may think in terms of killing 20 or 30 people. Religious sects are far less competent, but often have much grander ambitions." While Hoffman made this quote before September 11, 2001, it can still apply to many types of cults. . . . A number of cults have been involved in mass murder. Many other cults, although perhaps not causing as large a number of casualties, can still be very deadly.

For example, according to news reports, a cult called the Church of the First Born Lamb of God reportedly had a religious text titled *The Book of the New Covenant*. This book called for the slaying of any defectors from the church. Unfortunately, this is exactly what occurred. In 1988, killers gunned down a married couple who had defected from the group, and then shot and killed the couple's eight-year-old child. Soon afterward, the same killers murdered yet another cult defector. The police arrested the killers, and eventually they and the cult leader, Aaron LeBaron, received lengthy prison sentences. . . .

In addition to murder, though, cults have also occasionally resorted to kidnapping to keep their members from defecting. For example, after joining the Democratic Workers Party, a [U.S.] leftist cult, individuals found that getting out of the cult could be much more difficult than getting in. An article in *Redbook* about the cult states, "Those who tried to run away were often hunted down and dragged back to a 'safe house,' where they would be reindoctrinated under a kind of house arrest."

Karl Kahler, a former member of The Way International, tells in his book *The Cult That Snapped* about how The Way International formed a special squad of men whose job it was to attempt to "rescue" The Way members who had been grabbed off the street by deprogrammers (individuals who would kidnap and confine cult members and then attempt to force them to see the fallacies of the cult they belonged to). The leadership of The Way International, however, reportedly disbanded the group after a year because most of the members didn't want to come back to the group even when "rescued." They just wanted to get away from both the deprogrammers and their "rescuers."

Because many cult leaders have been found to manifest a large number of personality deficiencies and have often been diagnosed as psychopaths, they usually feel no empathy for the people they harm.

Abduction and Abuse

Occasionally, cults also kidnap people to get new members. According to *Time Asia*, a cult in China claims that Jesus Christ has returned to Earth in the form of a 30-year-old Chinese peasant woman, who has never been photographed and whose location is kept secret. The cult, called Lightning from the East, has been accused of kidnapping people and attempting to forcibly indoctrinate them into the cult. Individuals kidnapped by the cult claim to have been beaten, tortured, drugged, and sexually abused. When asked by reporters why the reborn Jesus, who supporters say has written a third book for the Bible, stays in hiding, a spokesperson for the cult said, "There's a time for secrecy and a time for openness, but she has her plan."

While the many incidents of murder and other serious crimes involving noncult victims are certainly startling, the most common victims of cults are the cult members themselves, who are often physically abused, sexually abused, psychologically abused, or suffer ill effects from poor sanitation and diet. According to Rutgers University [New Jersey] professor Benjamin Zablocki, cults are at high risk of becoming abusive to their members "because the members' adulation of ismatic leaders contributes to the leaders being corrupted by the power they seek and are accorded."

Readers should keep in mind that much of the damage inflicted on people by cults happens because, as Professor Zablocki points out, cults are formed almost exclusively for the benefit of the leader. Because many cult leaders have been found to manifest a large number of personality deficiencies and have often been diagnosed as psychopaths, they usually feel no empathy for the people they harm. Most cult leaders care only about being worshipped and obeyed, and about living a life of luxury.

"Psychopaths are social predators who charm, manipulate, and ruthlessly plow their way through life, leaving a broad trail of broken hearts, shattered expectations, and empty wallets," says Dr. Robert D. Hare in his book *Without Conscience: The Disturbing World of the Psychopaths Among Us.* "Completely lacking in conscience and feelings for others, they selfishly take what they want and do as they please, violating social norms and expectations without the slightest sense of guilt or regret."

Of all the types of harm that come from cults, however, the sexual abuse of cult members is a recurring theme that therapists hear over and over from cult members who have left groups and are attempting to recover. "Sexual abuse of women in cults is a pretty common story," says Lorna Goldberg, a cult expert and therapist. "Some groups demand celibacy, but either way cult leaders manipulate women sexually." A complaint heard many times from former members of cults that demand celibacy is that this restriction didn't apply to the cult leader, who often demanded sex from the members.

The Cult Child

Sexual abuse in cults, however, doesn't involve just females. It can also include males. And unfortunately, the sexual abuse of children within cults is much too common. It was well documented, for example, that Branch Davidian cult leader David Koresh [whose group died violently in Waco, Texas, in 1993] regularly had sex with underage females. There are many, many other examples.

On October 4, 2002, according to the *Atlanta Journal-Constitution* and other newspapers, a grand jury in Georgia handed down a 197-count indictment against Dwight York, leader of a cult called the United Nuwaubian Nation of Moors. These charges involve the sexual molestation of 13 children in the group, both boys and girls, ranging in age from 4 to 14.

"This has been the most voluminous case, in terms of number of counts, number of victims, and the sheer scope of the investigation that I've ever been associated with," said District Attorney Fred Bright. "I want the trial jury to hear the whole scope of the child molestation that happened here in Putnam County."

The approximately 1,000 members of the United Nuwaubian Nation of Moors live on a 476-acre plot in rural Putnam County, Georgia, while York, before his arrest, lived in a mansion nearby. With grandiosity typical of many cult leaders, York had reportedly planned to turn the commune into a nation separate from the United States called Egypt of the West. On October 25, 2002, York entered a plea of not guilty to all charges. However, his victims claim he told them that having sex with him was a religious ritual.

[Post-cult trauma syndrome] symptoms include spontaneous crying, depression, feelings of isolation, panic attacks, disassociation, difficulty concentrating, and low self-esteem.

"If we do that, we would go to heaven with the angels and we would never die," one of his young victims said York told her before molesting her. . . . [York later changed his plea to guilty and was sentenced for federal prison.]

Aftermath of Cult Membership

Psychologists and psychiatrists often find that, like the children, adult members of cults suffer not only physical and sexual abuse but also a number of psychological problems after spending time in a cult. These adult members often no longer have any friends other than cult members, and many of the thought-altering indoctrination techniques they underwent can negatively affect their ability to function in society after leaving the cult. Their time in the cult can lead to a condition known as post-cult trauma syndrome. Its symptoms include spontaneous crying, depression, feelings of isolation, panic attacks, disassociation, difficulty concentrating, and low self-esteem.

"I was a mental wreck," former cult member Maureen Dilley told me about her mental and emotional state after leaving a cult. "I believed I was crazy, and I had no friends or people to talk to."

"For a year I would just sit and cry," another former cult member told me. One former cult member became so depressed after leaving a cult he told me he tried to commit suicide by stepping in front of a bus.

The authors of the book *Cults and Psychological Abuse* [published by the American Family Foundation] state, "Clinical and research evidence suggests that many former members of abusive groups tend to blame themselves inappropriately for their problems, much as the group blamed them. Former members also tend to be depressed and anxious."

In a study of 43 people who had left a cult in Sweden, 93 percent reported anxiety and panic attacks, 91 percent reported difficulty handling emotions, 74 percent reported difficulty making decisions, 63 percent had suicidal thoughts (with 23 percent actually attempting suicide), and nearly half had psychosis-like symptoms. While some readers might argue that these results only came about because these individuals had mental problems before joining the cult, the study showed that only 16 percent of them had such problems.

2

Cults Are No More Violent than Other Religious Groups

David G. Bromley and J. Gordon Melton

David G. Bromley is a professor of sociology at Virginia Commonwealth University in Richmond and the University of Virginia in Charlottesville; his field of expertise is religious sociology and he is editor of the Journal for the Scientific Study of Religion. *J. Gordon Melton is founder and director of the Institute for the Study of American Religion, a research facility founded in 1969 in Evanston, Illinois. He is recognized as an expert on minority religions and has authored or coauthored over twenty books, including* New Religions: A Guide *and* Understanding New Religious Movements.

New religions, commonly called cults, are frequently perceived as more violent than well-established sects, but there are many reasons to question this stereotype. First, it is difficult to define the "new" elements that allegedly encourage violence because most "new" religions can trace their roots to established religions. Second, the number of violent groups is a very small percentage of the total number of new religious groups. Third, violent individuals and groups can be found in all religious and social categories, although in established religions the perpetrators are less likely to be seen as typical representatives of their faith. Finally, many mainstream religious leaders radiate the charisma commonly associated with cult leaders, but few of the former are automatically assumed to be encouraging violence; cult leaders are

*blamed for instigating violent tragedies even though their follow-
ers often act independently.*

The central misconception concerning new religions and
violence, and the one from which others most often derive, is that violence involving new religions is commonplace.
Implicit in this view is a contrast between new and established
religions, with the latter being depicted as more pacific. There
are a number of grounds for challenging the violence pervasiveness thesis.

First, there are few truly new religions. Most movements
labeled as new in fact borrow major ideological and organizational elements from long-established religious traditions that
are accorded social legitimacy. For example, Hare Krishna de-
rives from Bengali Hinduism; Aum Shinrikyô from Buddhism;
the Church Universal and Triumphant from Theosophy; the
Branch Davidians from Adventism; the United Order from
Mormonism; Happy, Healthy, Holy from Sikhism; Mahikari
from Shintoism; and ECKANKAR from [the Sanscrit-based
Indian religion] Sant Mat. In short, the criteria for distinguishing newness are much more complex than can be conveyed through any simple dichotomy.

Second, . . . , there are many forms of violence, and these
various types of violence may or may not be connected either
to a religious group or to a religious purpose. However, violent incidents, such as personal murder and suicide, are much
more likely to be connected to an individual with a new religious affiliation than to a member of an established church.
Further, violent incidents involving new religions are much
more newsworthy if they involve one of these movements.
The aggregation of all types of violence involving members of
new religions, attributions of acts to "cultic" qualities, and the
high-profile publicizing of such incidents creates the impression of pervasive violence. By contrast, violent or criminal acts
by members of mainstream religions usually are not attrib-

uted to their religious affiliation and, as the current revelations concerning pedophilia in the Catholic Church illustrate, violations of massive proportions are necessary to link religious organization and deviant behavior. With respect to the connection between new religions and violence, the reality is that since the murders committed by the [Charles] Manson Family some thirty years ago [1969], only twenty groups can be implicated in violent incidents involving multiple homicide or suicide. And most of these bear little resemblance to the stereotypical violent cult.

Conflicts involving [established religions] tend to be treated as political in nature, while those involving [new religions] tend to be defined as simply deviant or criminal.

Number of Groups vs. Number of Violent Groups

Third, the number of religious groups that have formed in recent decades is extraordinarily large. As [J. Gordon] Melton's [1998] compilation of religious groups reveals, more than half of the 2,000 religious groups now functioning in the United States were established since 1960. And these figures do not include the even larger number of movements, such as New Age groups, that are quasi-religious in nature. This means that the base on which any rate of violence involvement is calculated has become much larger and, given the relatively small number of violent incidents, the proportion involved in collective violence may be smaller. Whatever "age" is designated as the criterion for newness, it might be the case for the last half-century at least that the association of newness and violence actually is inverse. A similar conclusion can be reached for Africa, where more than 5,000 new religions have appeared over the last seventy years. The massive loss of life in the 2000 episode involving the Movement for the Restoration of the Ten Commandments [an Ugandan apocalyptic cult's mass suicide involving at least 800 fatalities] was horrific, but it was also a very rare event.

Fourth, even if schismatic religious groups and movements that constitute syncretic blends of several traditions are accepted as new, the comparative standard against which violence pervasiveness is measured is highly problematic. Even a cursory examination of the extent of religiously inspired violence around the globe reveals the untenability of distinguishing new from old religions in terms of their connection to violence. For example, at this writing there is ongoing violence between Protestants and Catholics in Northern Ireland, Israelis and Palestinians in the Middle East, Muslims and Hindus in India, Muslims and Christians in the Sudan, Christians and Muslims in Indonesia, and Tutsi and Bantu tribes in Rwanda. And this list could easily be extended. One reason that the comparison between new and established religions with respect to violence is elusive is that conflicts involving the latter tend to be treated as political in nature, while those involving the former tend to be defined as simply deviant or criminal. However, it would seem more insightful to interpret the resistance that new religious movements offer to the established order as political, albeit through a religious format. Viewed from this perspective, mainline churches in the United States, for example, currently are in a pacific period during which their political alliance with the state and other major institutions is relatively strong, supportive, and stable. However, the histories of many denominations are replete with much more confrontive stances involving resistance and repression. And as conflicts in recent decades over issues like race relations, abortion, and governmental authority indicate, religious groups that appear settled may quickly reassume a more confrontive posture.

Violence Pervasiveness Theory Based on Illogical Definitions

In sum, the violence pervasiveness thesis is rooted in problematic definitions of newness and violence that load the argument in the direction of its confirmation. It tends to be based on the visibility given to deviant activity by new religions. And finally, it gains support by largely ignoring or redefining violence in which established religions have been and are involved.

The argument that violence by new religions is pervasive leads naturally to the question of why this might be so. The answer is often traced to the premise that these movements are inherently violence prone. By this logic, a "tendency toward violence" becomes a defining characteristic of new religions and is attributed to instability and pathological organizational and leadership qualities.... [C]harismatic leadership [is among the characteristics often] posited as sources of movement instability that creates a tendency toward violence.

Fresh outbursts of charisma always pose a threat to established social patterns, and at the same time charisma is a potent form of authority that can generate intense commitment. As a result, there are countervailing pressures to preserve and routinize its effects in many religious traditions. Because charisma can easily outflank institutional control mechanisms, traditions in which charisma is an important resource recount cautionary tales of its dangers and abuse. In the Christian tradition, accounts of the pathological, in this case violent, religious leader can be traced to sixteenth-century Germany during a period of developing hostilities between Roman Catholics and Lutherans. Two radical movements of the time, one led by the priest Thomas Münzer and the other by the prophet Jan Bokelson at the town of Münster, took up arms against civil authorities; both movements were crushed and their leaders executed. However, in both Roman Catholic and Lutheran retelling of these sagas, Münzer and Münster came to symbolize the dangers of charismatic leadership and of following such leaders. In these cases, of course, we lack the detailed historical records necessary to determine the extent of instigation and provocation on either side, but it is clear that a small number of historical cases have been invoked to confirm the connection between charismatic leadership and violence. In the present era, Jim Jones [who followers committed mass suicide] and Charles Manson (despite the contested status of the Manson Family as religious group) serve as comparable cultural landmarks.

> *It is problematic to assert a direct causal relationship between charismatic leadership and violence.*

Mainstream Charismatics

The problem with selecting specific instances in which charismatic leaders may have provoked their followers to violent confrontations, of course, is the prevalence of charisma in religious and nonreligious settings alike. Since a high proportion of new religious movements begin with a charismatic leader and a small band of followers, and since most established religious groups often preserve a measure of charismatic authority, it is problematic to assert a direct causal relationship between charismatic leadership and violence. For example, a number of religious leaders associated with established religious groups have been regarded as extremely charismatic—Billy Graham (Southern Baptist), Oral Roberts (United Methodist), Fulton Sheen (Roman Catholic), and Jimmy Swaggart (Assemblies of God). Some are respected and others reproved, but they are not immediately presumed to harbor violent tendencies. Further, the presence of charismatic leadership does not establish a causal link to specific outcomes. For example, in the cases of both the Peoples Temple [Jim Jones's organization] and Rajneesh [a spiritual enlightenment group involved in a 1984 mass poisoning attempt in Oregon, and several smaller murder plots], it was organizational lieutenants who were pivotal in the initiation of violence, the high profile of Bhagwan [Shree Rajneesh] and Jim Jones notwithstanding. . . . Attributing organizational outcomes to the personality of a single individual, even a powerful charismatic leader, usually camouflages much more complex social dynamics.

3

Cults Brainwash
Their Members

Margaret Thaler Singer

Margaret Thaler Singer is a clinical psychologist and an emeritus adjunct professor at the University of California, Berkeley. A recognized expert on cults and on post-traumatic stress, she is the coauthor (with Janja Lalich) of "Crazy" Therapies.

The drastic personality changes and irrational actions apparent in many cult members are induced by the cults through "thought reform," a type of brainwashing that attacks a person's sense of self through subtle manipulation and the fostering of dependency. Rather than the imprisonment and torture commonly associated with "brainwashing," thought reform programs use soft-sell methods, which break down resistance so gradually that the victim is unaware how drastically he or she is changing. While many recruits successfully resist or recover, thought reform is nonetheless highly effective and highly dangerous. Most of the cult leaders who employ these methods are con artists or psychopaths, concerned only with using others toward unscrupulous ends.

People repeatedly ask me how cult leaders get their followers to do such things as give their wives to a child-molesting cult leader, drop out of medical school to follow a martial arts guru, give several million dollars to a self-appointed messiah who wears a wig and has his favorite women dress like Jezebel, or practice sexual abstinence while following a blatantly promiscuous guru. Because of the great discrepancies between individuals' conduct before cult membership and the behavior exhibited while in the cult, families, friends, and the public wonder how these changes in attitude and behavior are induced.

How cult leaders and other clever operators get people to do their bidding seems arcane and mysterious to most persons, but I find there is nothing esoteric about it at all. There are no secret drugs or potions. It is just words and group pressures, put together in packaged forms. Modern-day manipulators use methods of persuasion employed since the days of the cavemen, but the masterful con artists of today have hit upon a way to put the techniques together in packages that are especially successful. As a result, thought reform, as a form of influence and persuasion, falls on the extreme end of a continuum that also includes education as we typically see it, advertising, propaganda, and indoctrination.

[Thought reform programs] undermine [the cult member's] basic consciousness, reality awareness, beliefs and worldview, emotional control, and defense mechanisms.

There is a mistaken notion that thought reform can only be carried out in confined places and under threat of physical torture or death. But it is important to remember that the brainwashing programs of the forties and fifties [which began in China and spread to other Communist countries] were applied not only to military or civilian prisoners of war but also to the general population. In all our research, I and others who study these programs emphasize over and over that imprisonment and overt violence are not necessary and are actually counterproductive when influencing people to change their attitudes and behaviors. If one really wants to influence others, various coordinated soft-sell programs are cheaper, less obvious, and highly effective. The old maxim "Honey gathers more flies than vinegar" remains true today.

Attacking the Self

There is, however, an important distinction to be made between the version of thought reform prevalent in the 1940s and 1950s and the version used by a number of contemporary groups, including cults, large group awareness training programs, and assorted other groups. These latter-day efforts have built upon the age-old influence techniques to perfect amazingly successful programs of persuasion and change. What's new—and crucial—is that these programs change attitudes by attacking essential aspects of a person's sense of self, unlike the earlier brainwashing programs that primarily confronted a person's political beliefs.

Today's programs are designed to destabilize an individual's sense of self by undermining his or her basic consciousness, reality awareness, beliefs and worldview, emotional control, and defense mechanisms. This attack on a person's central stability, or self-concept, and on a person's capacity for self-evaluation is the principal technique that makes the newer programs work. Moreover, this attack is carried out under a variety of guises and conditions—and rarely does it include forced confinement or direct physical coercion. Rather, it is a subtle and powerful psychological process of destabilization and induced dependency.

Thankfully, these programs do not change people permanently. Nor are they 100 percent effective. Cults are not all alike, thought-reform programs are not all alike, and not everyone exposed to specific intense influence processes succumbs and follows the group. Some cults try to defend themselves by saying, in effect, "See, not everyone joins or stays, so we must not be using brainwashing techniques." Many recruits do succumb, however, and the better organized the influence processes used, the more people will succumb.

What is of concern, then, is that certain groups and training programs that have emerged in the last half century represent well-organized, highly orchestrated influence efforts that are widely successful in recruiting and converting people under certain conditions for certain ends. My interest has been in how these processes work, in the psychological and social techniques that produce these behavioral and attitudinal changes. I am less interested in whether the content of the group centers around religion, psychology, self-improvement politics, life-style, or flying saucers. I am more interested in the widespread use of brainwashing techniques by crooks, swindlers, psychopaths, and egomaniacs of every sort.

How Thought Reform Works

Brainwashing is not experienced as a fever or a pain might be; it is in invisible social adaptation. When you are the subject of it, you are not aware of the intent of the influence processes that are going on, and especially, you are not aware of the changes taking place within you.

In his memoirs, Cardinal Mindszenty [former head of the Roman Catholic Church in Hungary, who was subjected to thought reform in the 1950s] wrote, "Without knowing what had happened to me, I had become a different person." And when asked about being brainwashed, [newspaper heiress] Patty Hearst said, "The strangest part of all this, however, as the SLA [Symbionese Liberation Army, the revolutionary cult that abducted her in 1974] delighted in informing me later, was that they themselves were surprised at how docile and trusting I had become. . . . It was also true, I must admit, that the thought of escaping from them later simply never entered my mind. I had become convinced that there was no possibility of escape. . . . I suppose I could have walked out of the apartment and away from it all, but I didn't. It simply never occurred to me."

A thought-reform program is not a one-shot event but a gradual process of breaking down and transformation. It can be likened to gaining weight, a few ounces, a half pound, a pound at a time. Before long, without even noticing the initial changes—we are confronted with a new physique. So, too, with brainwashing. A twist here, a tweak there—and there it is: a new psychic attitude, a new mental outlook. These systematic manipulations of social and psychological influences under particular conditions are called *programs* because the means by which change is brought about is coordinated. And it is because the changes cause the learning and adoption of a certain set of attitudes, usually accompanied by a certain set of behaviors, that the effort and the result are called *thought reform*.

Thus, thought reform is a concerted effort to change a person's way of looking at the world, which will change his or her behavior. It is distinguished from other forms of social learning by the conditions under which it is conducted and by the techniques of environmental and interpersonal manipulation that are meant to suppress certain behavior and to elicit and train other behavior. And it does not consist of only one program—there are many ways and methods to accomplish it.

4

Mass Suicide Can Be the Logical Outcome of a Cult's Religious Belief

Dereck Daschke and W. Michael Ashcraft

Dereck Daschke and W. Michael Ashcraft both teach at Truman State University in Missouri: Daschke is an assistant professor of philosophy, Ashcraft an associate professor of religion. Ashcraft is also the author of The Dawn of the New Cycle: Point Loma Theosophists and American Culture *and a former chairman of the New Religious Movements Group of the American Academy of Religion.*

The approach of the "new millennium" seemed to bring out the doomsday mentality in religion in the late 1990s, a mentality that at its most dangerous extreme manifested itself in group suicides and mass murders—the release of poison gas in Tokyo, the 1995 Oklahoma City bombing, the 1997 suicide of thirty-nine Heaven's Gate members. Less violent groups, such as Chen Tao (which predicted the appearance of God in Texas in 1998), and many religious commentators inspired by the Y2K panic shared the idea that modern society was hopelessly corrupt and the end of the world imminent, attitudes that only intensify despair and fatalism.

The concept of a new millennium—a literal or symbolic thousand-year reign of peace that follows a catastrophic, global tribulation—proffered by the [Biblical] Book of Revela-

Dereck Daschke and W. Michael Ashcraft, eds., *New Religious Movements: A Documentary Reader*. New York: New York University Press, 2005, pp. 297–302. Copyright © 2005 by New York University. All rights reserved. Reproduced by permission of the publisher and the authors.

tion can be attached to any date, or no date. And yet, at the end of the twentieth century, it became inextricably associated with what should have been a prophetically innocuous year in the Gregorian calendar: the year 2000. Such is the power of the phrase "a new millennium" that apocalyptic interest and expectation increased palpably in the latter half of the 1990s, a "millennial stew" fueled by, and probably itself fueling, an explosion of dark predictions from pulpits, a rash of apocalyptically themed movies, television shows, and pop songs, and an apparent rise in "doomsday cults."

While the aftermath of the 1993 Branch Davidian inferno lingered, another shocking event occurred on March 20, 1995. A Japanese apocalyptic group, Aum Shinrikyo, released deadly sarin gas into Tokyo's subway system, killing twelve people and injuring thousands. The next month, on the anniversary of the destruction of the Branch Davidian community in Waco [Texas], Timothy McVeigh killed 168 people when he blew up the federal building in Oklahoma City. While it was clearly an earlier date that motivated McVeigh, the leader of Aum Shinrikyo, Shoko Asahara, apparently expected Armageddon in 2000—the sarin attack was to serve both as a pre-emptive strike against an irredeemably evil and corrupt world (even as it was meant to be a merciful release from it for its victims) and as a distraction for police, who planned to raid Aum's headquarters.

To the Class, [ritual death] was not suicide, but liberation—it was the rest of humanity who had chosen death by staying in this world.

An Increasingly Unstable World Order

Baseless or not, it was difficult for many to disassociate this increase in religious violence from the advent of a "new millennium" and all of the imagery wedded to that phrase. Moreover, with the end of the Cold War and the dismantling of the Soviet Union, what had once been a clear moral and political order in the world was gone, and some of the stances that had defined America for decades became moot. Although the memory of nuclear threat was still fresh, it was no longer many people's worst fear, especially when so many other crises—AIDS, global warming, urban decay—loomed. What should have been a period of relative security and peace for most Americans was often fraught with a sense of anxiety and purposelessness. Events such as those in Oklahoma City and Tokyo seemed only to confirm their worst suspicions—that the world itself was coming unmoored. On the other hand, to countless Christians, these conditions offered a strange hope: they could be read as signs that the events depicted in the Book of Revelation had commenced. Here we examine two NRMs [new religious movements] that had a very different take on the eschatological significance of the state of the world in general and of the year 2000 in particular.

Heaven's Gate was a San Diego group with a keen interest in the coming millennial change and other aspects of the Endtimes. Like Aum Shinrikyo, they saw human existence itself as evil and intolerable and sought to escape to "The Evolutionary Level Above Human" (referred to as "T.E.L.A.H."). However, their beliefs did not prompt the group to inflict death on others, but rather on themselves: on March 26, 1997, thirty-nine members of Heaven's Gate were found to have killed themselves in a ritualistic fashion; it was the largest mass suicide in American history. "The Class," as they called themselves, wore black pajamas, Nike running shoes, and plastic bags over their heads—presumably to help accelerate the effect of the sleeping pills and alcohol on which they had overdosed. To the Class, this was not suicide, but liberation—it was the rest of humanity who had chosen death by staying in this world.

Heaven's Gate Theology

According to Marshall Herff Applewhite (1931–1997), who had formed the group (then called "Human Individual Metamorphosis" or HIM) in the early 1970s with Bonnie Lu Nettles (1927–1985), the universe as we know it was created as an experimental testing ground for souls to prepare for the next stage of cosmic evolution, T.E.L.A.H. But the experiment had failed, and the earth had long since been controlled by wicked aliens they called the Luciferians. Heaven's Gate members saw themselves as the current incarnations of the souls of Jesus and the early Christian church and thus were the few souls advanced enough to transcend to T.E.L.A.H. with the assistance of the good aliens and their spacecraft. When a photo of the Hale-Bopp comet appeared on the Internet in November 1996 with what was purported to be a Saturn-shaped flying saucer following close behind, this seemed to Applewhite and the Class to be their chance to escape. That the photo was shown to be a hoax could not dissuade them, as they defiantly stated on their Website just prior to their deaths.

According to Chen ... the life forces of all material things, animate and inanimate, would become alive and potentially agitated and vengeful.

The specter of mass suicide also haunted another apocalyptic group awaiting planetary escape by way of UFO, if only in the media's portrayal of it, but on this point it could not have been more different from Heaven's Gate. Chen Tao ("True Way") of Taiwan expected 1999 to be the beginning of a forty-four-year Great Tribulation. This year would be marked by "Noah's Flood" in Eastern Asia, the massacre of "a thousand million" Taiwanese by "devil spirits" who possess people and feed off their "spiritual light energy" and, ultimately, a Chinese nuclear attack on Taiwan. They were led by Master Hon-ming Chen (b. 1956), a former professor of social science who had a lifelong history of religious revelation, first by communicating with God through visions of golden balls of light, later by gazing into a ring worn backwards on his hand. In 1995 it was revealed to him that North America was the "Pure Land of God" and that he and his followers must move there to prepare for the end of the current world cycle. According to Chen's writings, *The Practical Evidence and Study of the World of God and Buddha* (1996) and *God's Descending in Clouds (Flying Saucers) on Earth to Save People* (1997), the earth had been destroyed before in five previous Great Tribulations, the karmic effects of the actions of "Heavenly Devil Kings." In each case, God had saved only the inhabitants of North America, rescuing them in flying saucers.

Chen Tao Prepares for the Tribulation

In 1997, Chen Tao (also known as the God Saves the Earth Flying Saucer Foundation) established God's Salvation Church in San Dimas, California, then scouted locations for the other churches necessary to carry out its work of alerting North Americans to the coming Tribulation. They also sought the reincarnations of Jesus and the Buddha, finding them in the course of their travels in the form of two young boys who were brought into the group. One hundred and fifty members settled in Garland, Texas, which Chen said was an auspicious place, as the name sounded like "God's Land," and which he declared to be the location where God would appear in person to prepare North Americans for their imminent salvation. According to Chen, as the Tribulation approached, the life forces of all material things, animate and inanimate, would become alive and potentially agitated and vengeful. If one did not wish to experience the wrath of these "spirits" in the coming year, it would be best to be compassionate toward everything in one's life, especially by becoming vegan or vegetarian.

Chen Tao members not only opposed suicide as karmically detrimental, but they also opposed harming any living creature, a stance the worldwide media—whom Chen invited to witness his frequent revelatory pronouncements—found difficult to reconcile with the "UFO/suicide cult" identification with which the group had been saddled, due to apparent parallels with Heaven's Gate. Leading up to and including March 31, 1998, when Chen Tao members expected God's physical appearance in Garland, reporters hounded Chen about plans for a mass suicide if God failed to appear. Chen routinely deflected this line of questioning, but on this last date, he attempted to demonstrate that he was, at that time, in fact God in a physical body by staring into the sun. Reporters and many members were unconvinced, and when Chen moved the group again to Lockport, New York, to await divine rescue, only about thirty of the roughly one-hundred and fifty Garland members came with him. After 1999 passed without incident, Chen determined that God, in his mercy, had spared the world temporarily, and Chen continued his wait with a handful of devoted followers for God's flying saucers to take the North Americans from their doomed planet and place them on Mars, in the fourth dimension.

To a great extent, an expansive, fantastic—even magical—vision of science and technology is the uniting aspect of these three movements.

Y2K and Cult Thinking

Ironically, arguably the most legitimate threat of destruction of the world as we know it due to the calendrical change of the new millennium came from a thoroughly secular and modern source: the computer. Due to memory constraints on the first computers, recording years was restricted to two digits (65 for 1965, for example); this shortcut remained standard practice even as vastly improved storage capacity made the personal computing revolution of the 1980s possible. As the millennial change-over loomed, however, many in the programming industry feared that the temporally illogical backward step from "99" to "00" would cause many systems to crash, including those in some of the world's most vital sectors: banking, transportation, energy delivery, military defense—just about every system of any importance contained an outdated microchip somewhere.

In the 1990s, a massive global effort was launched to head off this "Y2K" ("Year 2000") crisis, but many believed it was too little, too late. Several influential religious observers saw something else in the potential collapse of modern society at the hands of its own vaunted technology: the fulfillment of biblical prophecy and the opportunity for Christ return triumphantly to a humanity humbled by the devastation of its "perfectible," scientifically based society. . . . The glee with which some of these prophets of doom predicted the destruction of society in the course of a global computer malfunction did not prevent many of them from posting their warnings on the Internet. . . .

Cults and Science

To a great extent, an expansive, fantastic—even magical— vision of science and technology is the uniting aspect of these three movements. In the cases of Heaven's Gate and Chen Tao, besides borrowing the UFO concept from popular culture and science fiction, members of both groups saw a certain kind of "scientism" as capable of expressing spiritual truths. Applewhite described many of his cosmological concepts in terms of the television series *Star Trek*. In its first incarnation as the Soul Light Resurgence Association in Taiwan, Chen Tao members measured spiritual light energy with electronic equipment, not unlike the E-meters [purported mind-reading lie detectors] of Scientology. These forms of "scientific" knowledge dovetail with both groups' adoption of flying saucer ideologies. . . . Such beliefs seem to expand one's vision and breadth of knowledge of the universe, making it impossible to see it as others do.

The science and technology at the root of the Y2K scare ironically come across to many Americans as just as alien as

UFOs. Yet for the prophetically minded, the warnings about the possible collapse of the computerized information network were signs to the righteous concerning the secrets of the Endtimes, offering comfort that the Reign of Christ was at hand and warning them to prepare for the coming upheaval. Yet the Y2K movement differs from the two UFO groups discussed here in that, whereas the latter expected to leave Earth and literally go to a new world, many in the former thought that a computer glitch would bring about the "end of the world as we know it," which some believed could trigger Armageddon and usher in the Messianic age. Hence much of the fascination with Y2K among conservative Christians stemmed from their longstanding war against modern, secular society, which they expected to be soon hoisted on its own technological petard, ushering in the New Society of God's Kingdom. While not overly emphasized, Chen Tao's interest in "soul light" as well as basic Buddhist conceptualizations of selfhood suggest an aspect of New Self appeal for its members. On the other hand, Heaven's Gate members felt such antagonism toward humanness that they subsumed the self entirely, eradicating their gender through surgical castration and by adopting names such as "Srrody," and ultimately leaving behind their human "vessels" as they sought the next evolutionary level. As communal groups, however, both Heaven's Gate and Chen Tao created alternative New Societies as they awaited the great transformation that would leave the current ones, and the world that produced them, behind.

5

Authorities Provoke Some Cult Mass Deaths

William Norman Grigg

William Norman Grigg is a senior editor and longtime contributor to The New American.

One of the most commonly cited example of cults' presumed tendency towards mass violence is the 1993 case of the Branch Davidians in Waco, Texas, whose seven-week standoff against federal agents of the Bureau of Alcohol, Tobacco and Firearms (ATF) culminated in a paramilitary raid, the release of tear gas, and a fire that killed seventy-six cult members. Yet government agents, whose stated intent was to look into the cult's alleged stockpiling of weapons, was more to blame for the tragedy than was the cult. Subsequent investigation proved that claims about the cult's violent tendencies and "warfare mentality" were greatly exaggerated, based on anti-cult prejudice and unsubstantiated rumors. Such prejudices inflame situations involving cults to provoke needless tragedy.

Ten years ago on February 28th [1993], the Bureau of Alcohol, Tobacco and Firearms (ATF) staged an armed raid against the Branch Davidian community outside of Waco, Texas. Four ATF agents and six Branch Davidians perished needlessly in that eminently avoidable shootout.

But those tragic deaths merely foreshadowed the hideous events of April 19th: The prolonged gassing of the Davidians'

William Norman Grigg, "Waco Revisited: The Horrifying Liquidation of Waco's Branch Davidian Sect, Which Began with an ATF Raid 10 Years ago, Displayed Our Government's Capacity for Lethal Lawlessness," *The New American*, vol. 19, February 24, 2003. Copyright © 2003 American Opinion Publishing Incorporated. Reproduced by permission.

church complex by the FBI; the ensuing fire that enveloped the complex; and the horrifying spectacle—captured on forward-looking infrared tape—of federal paramilitaries directing automatic weapons fire into the burning complex, cutting off avenues of possible retreat.

The federal assault on the Branch Davidians actually began on February 27th, when the *Waco Tribune-Herald* published the first installment of a seven-part piece on David Koresh and his followers. Built largely on accusations from disaffected former Davidians, the series depicted Koresh as a sexually depraved, potentially violent megalomaniac and his followers as hopelessly deluded cultists. Three of the individuals interviewed in the newspaper series were working with ATF Special Agent Davy Aguilera, and executives of the *Tribune-Herald* had discussed the series with the ATF prior to publication.

The opening installment, observes Texas journalist Dick Reavis in his study *The Ashes of Waco*, "was accompanied by an editorial scolding local lawmen—but not mentioning the feds—for having turned a blind eye to goings-on at Mount Carmel, perhaps because its composers knew that federal action was at hand." Prior to the raid, ATF public relations director Sharon Wheeler had contacted local reporters to arrange a February 28th press conference—presumably to announce the ATF's triumphant armed raid against "cult leader" Koresh and his heavily armed followers.

The Curtain Rises

The Branch Davidians were indeed "stockpiling" firearms as part of a perfectly legal retail trade. The ATF insisted that the February 28th raid was a pre-emptive strike intended to prevent the Davidians from becoming a danger to the local community. However, as ATF Director Stephen Higgins would later admit, a lengthy investigation of the group's firearms dealings failed to produce probable cause for a search.

It wasn't until mid-February that the key "evidence" was found. David Kopel and Paul Blackman point out in their definitive study *No More Wacos*: "The key evidence in BATF Director Higgins' mind—based on his testimony before the House Judiciary Committee—appears to have been Koresh's religious views, pro-gun rights views, criticism of federal gun laws, and hostility toward the BATF, all of which were protected by the First Amendment." After the lethal ATF raid, the agency obtained a second warrant to seize audio and videotapes documenting negative views "of firearms law enforcement and particularly the Bureau of Alcohol, Tobacco and Firearms" as "evidence [of Koresh's] or other cult members' motive for wanting to shoot and kill ATF agents."

In fact, Koresh—however bizarre his religious beliefs, however objectionable his sexual conduct—had gone to great lengths to prevent an armed confrontation with the ATF. In congressional testimony, a gun dealer who had sold weapons to Koresh described a late 1992 visit from ATF investigators concerned about the Davidians' gun inventory. When the dealer informed Koresh over the phone of the agents' concerns, Koresh responded by inviting the agents to Mount Carmel to examine his gun inventory and paperwork. The ATF agents declined the offer.

A few hours before the ATF raid, Koresh had learned it was coming (thanks, in large measure, to the ATF's juvenile eagerness to cue in local journalists). Just prior to the shootout, Koresh had a conversation with ATF informant Robert Rodriguez, who had lived at Mount Carmel for a short time. Anticipating the worst, Rodriguez expected to get "a bullet in the back," he later recalled. If Koresh had been the maniacal terrorist subsequently portrayed in federal propaganda, Rodriguez would have been a valuable hostage. Instead, Koresh simply said "Good luck, Robert," shook the informant's hand, and let him go in peace. When Rodriguez reached the ATF command post, he warned the raid commander, Charles Sarabyn: "Chuck, they know. They know."

Rather than calling off the raid, Sarabyn quizzed Rodriguez about the Davidians' battle plans: Did he see any weapons? Were the Davidians mobilizing? Rodriguez answered no. Well then, Sarabyn persisted, what were the Davidians doing when he left? "They were praying," Rodriguez replied. If Sarabyn had any misgivings about shooting up a church full of women and children at prayer, he manfully shoved them aside and did what he took to be his duty.

The ATF paramilitaries displayed little concern about the supposed threat from the Davidians. They pulled up to Mount Carmel on flat-bed trucks, offering an incredibly vulnerable target. Jeff Jamar, who served as FBI commander at Waco, admitted to Justice Department investigators that the Davidians "could have easily killed all of those [ATF] agents before they even got out of the cattle cars with the kind of weapons they had." Yet the Davidians withheld that deadly fusillade, a curious tactical decision for a group purportedly conspiring to murder federal agents.

Not only did the ATF expect to stage a "dynamic entry" at Mount Carmel, they hadn't even rehearsed a peaceful entry.

More curious still, was David Koresh's final, desperate attempt to prevent the shootout. Davidian survivors testify that Koresh opened the front door to the Mount Carmel complex and urged the Feds to hold their fire. According to the Davidians, this petition was met with gunfire—the opening salvo in what would become an agonizing 51-day standoff ending in the immolation of nearly 80 innocent human beings on April 19th.

Going Off-script

The ATF's script was simple: The agents would mount a straight power play, swarming Mount Carmel, flinging "flash-bang" charges into the building to disorient its occupants, and seizing Koresh and his associates. Not only did the ATF expect to stage a "dynamic entry" at Mount Carmel, they hadn't even rehearsed a peaceful entry. ATF raider Kenneth King was asked in court: "Even if . . . the people at the front door had been welcomed in by David Koresh, none of that would have made any difference, as far as what you were doing was concerned?" "No, sir," replied King.

In fact, the ATF expected casualties, including civilian deaths. Note Kopel and Blackman: "The fall 1993 Treasury investigation into BATF conduct at Waco offers no indication that BATF raid planners were concerned about—or even discussed—how different arrest strategies might minimize the risk of possible injury or death to innocent civilians, including the children. An Army memo compiled in anticipation of the February 28th raid noted that the BATF 'recognizes that casualties are probable. . . . Casualties will be the [BATF], bad guys and civilians.'"

The Davidians, however, weren't content to play their scripted role. Under an unprovoked assault, they properly responded with lethal force of their own. Every one of the 10 deaths that terrible morning was a tragedy, but those tragedies would never have occurred if the ATF had not launched the illegal raid in the first place. In fact, the death toll would certainly have been much higher if the Davidians had been bent on slaughter rather than self-defense. In keeping with the Christian principles governing the use of deadly force, they allowed the defeated raiders to retreat, rather than mowing them down once the tide of battle had turned and the Feds were at their mercy.

Why?

What prompted the ATF to stage the Mount Carmel raid? Why did the agency decide that open gunplay was its only option? David Koresh had expressed willingness to cooperate with the ATF. If it was considered dangerous to arrest Koresh at Mount Carmel, he could easily have been arrested during his frequent visits to Waco, or while jogging outside the complex. In fact, shortly before the raid, Koresh went target shooting with two ATF agents. Why, then, did the ATF choose to mount a military strike?

One obvious reason is that the ATF wanted to stage a made-for-television event that would enhance the agency's tarnished image. In December 1992, the ATF came under political fire because of a *60 Minutes* investigation of sexual harassment within the department. What better way to recapture the PR initiative than by staging a daring raid on a heavily armed "cult compound"?

This atrocity was committed on American soil by our own government.

"A BATF memo written two days before the February 28, 1993, raid explained, 'this operation will generate considerable attention, both locally (Texas) and nationally,'" observe Kopel and Blackman. "BATF public relations director Sharon Wheeler called reporters to ask them for their weekend phone numbers. The reporters contend, and Wheeler denies, that she asked them if they would be interested in covering a weapons raid on a 'cult.' The ATF's arrogant confidence that it could pull off its violent PR stunt is captured in the codename for the February 28th attack—'Showtime.'"

Within hours of the Mount Carmel shootout, the FBI took over the siege. For more than a month and a half, the FBI—with the expert advice of Igor Smirnov of the Moscow Institute of Psycho-correction—conducted a campaign of psychological torture designed to break the will of the Davidians.

On the morning of April 19th, FBI operatives and Delta Force commandos staged a combined armor and infantry raid after relentlessly pumping CS gas into the Mount Carmel church building. (The U.S. military is forbidden by treaty to use on the battlefield the specific chemical agent used against American citizens at Waco.) Around noon, a fire began that quickly enveloped the church. Seventy-six people, including 17 small children, were cremated in the fire. Shockingly, a recorded radio transmission between FBI commander Jamar and Dick Rogers, commander of the Bureau's Hostage Rescue Team, indicates that Jamar intended for the adult Davidians to perish in the flames.

Never Forget

This atrocity was committed on American soil by our own government. It grew out of a campaign to "pre-empt" David Koresh's alleged efforts to obtain supposedly illegal firearms. That rationale is curiously similar to that invoked by the Bush administration to justify its desire to wage a "preemptive" war against Iraq, before Saddam Hussein acquires "weapons of mass destruction."

In the build-up to another war on Iraq, the Bush administration and its apologists remind us that Saddam used chemical weapons against his own population. But there is little public recognition that our own government did pretty much the same thing on the morning of April 19, 1993. Of course, the United States is not Iraq. Despite our government's abuses of power such as Waco, many of our freedoms are still largely intact, unlike those of the Iraqi people suffering under Saddam's murderous and oppressive regime. But Waco offers a potent illustration of the U.S. government's own capacity for lethal lawlessness, when the custodians of liberty—"We the people," acting through our elected representatives—fail to remain vigilant.

The 10th anniversary is a timely reminder that the government we should worry about most is not headquartered in Baghdad, Pyongyang, Teheran, or Beijing—but in Washington, D.C. If, God forbid, we lose our freedom, it will be because we authored our own destruction.

6

Cults Are Corruptions of Legitimate Religions

Ron Rhodes

Ron Rhodes is founder and president of Reasoning from the Scriptures Ministries, a Christian nonprofit corporation dedicated to practical biblical theology. A former editor of the Christian Research Newsletter, *he has written over a dozen books, including* The Culting of America. *He is also an adjunct professor of theology at Biola University in California, Southern Evangelical Seminary in North Carolina, and Golden Gate Seminary in California.*

All religious cults can trace their roots to established religions and many claim to still follow the parent religion, but cults adopt corrupt doctrines incompatible with their parent faiths. Among the most common characteristics of a cult is the claim to "new revelations" that supersede long-established scriptures and seem to be adjusted at the convenience of the cult. All cults defer to their sect's scriptures over the parent religion's, even claiming that the originals can never be properly understood apart from the new.

It is for good reason that every book in the [Christian Bible's] New Testament except Philemon has something to say about false teachers, false prophets, false gospels, or heresies. Jesus Himself sternly warned His followers to watch out for false prophets and false Christs. The apostle Paul warned

Ron Rhodes, *The Challenge of the Cults and New Religions*. Grand Rapids, MI: Zondervan, 2001, pp. 19–25. Copyright © 2001 by Ron Rhodes. Used by permission of Zondervan.

of a different Jesus, a different spirit, false apostles, and those who preach "another gospel". First John 4:1 understandably urges believers to "test the spirits." The concern is obvious: *Counterfeit prophets who speak of a counterfeit Christ who preaches a counterfeit gospel can yield only a counterfeit salvation.* Because there are eternal consequences to false teachings, Scripture bears numerous warnings.

With that in mind, we can see that a study of the various cults in our midst should be a high priority for us all. But before we can focus attention on specific cults, we must be clear on what a "cult" is. This is a seemingly formidable task. Talk to 10 different cult "experts" and you may well be given 10 different definitions. Sociologists have their opinions (authoritarianism and exclusivism play big roles in their thinking), psychologists have their opinions (mind-control is a big issue with them), and theologians have their opinions (heretical doctrines are the main issue of concern). Still others, like journalists and reporters, often focus on the more sensational elements of the cults, such as mass suicides and bizarre rituals and practices.

What Exactly Is a Cult?

Some people today say we shouldn't even use the term *cult* because it carries such negative connotations. Instead, they prefer terms like "new religions" or "alternative religions." While I understand this viewpoint, I think it is legitimate to use the term *cult*. I want to emphasize, though, that when I use the term I do not intend it as a pejorative, inflammatory, or injurious word. . . . I use the term simply as means of categorizing certain religious or semi-religious groups in the world.

Our English word *cult* comes from the Latin word *cultus*, which means "worship." Linguistically a cultic action is one that involves external rites and ceremonies with a worshipful attitude on the part of the devotee. A "cult" in this sense refers to a system of worship distinguishable from others. Of course, the modern usage of the word is much more specific than this linguistic definition.

In modern times, the term *cult* has primarily been defined from both sociological and theological perspectives. Those who opt for the sociological definition say that a cult is a religious or semi-religious sect or group whose members are controlled or dominated almost entirely by a single individual or organization. This definition generally includes (but is not limited to) the authoritarian, manipulative; and sometimes communal features of cults. Cults that fall into this category include the Hare Krishnas, the Children of God (The Family), and the Unification Church.

While I believe we gain some very important insights on the cultic mentality from sociology . . . my long experience in dealing with cultists has convinced me that it is more accurate to define a cult from a theological perspective. As one cult observer put it, "Sociological, psychological, and journalistic observations sometimes show us the human dynamics that frequently result from a cult belief system, but they are not sufficient Christian foundations for determining a group's status *as* a cult." Therefore, I believe the best policy is to define a cult theologically, but we can then gain some key insights into the cultic mentality from sociology and psychology.

Various Theological Definitions

The problem is how to word a theological definition of a cult. What specific components should make up this definition? Different cult experts have offered different opinions.

Gordon Lewis, in his book *Confronting the Cults*, suggests that the term *cult* "designates a religious group which claims authorization by Christ and the Bible, but neglects or distorts the gospel—the central message of the Savior and the Scripture." James Sire, author of *Scripture Twisting*, suggests that a cult is "any religious movement that is organizationally distinct and has doctrines and/or practices that contradict those of the Scriptures as interpreted by traditional Christianity as represented by the major Catholic and Protestant denominations, and as expressed in such statements as the Apostles' Creed."

My late colleague Walter Martin defined a cult this way:

> By "cult," we mean a group, religious in nature, which surrounds a leader or a group of teachings which either denies or misinterprets essential biblical doctrine. Most cults have a single leader, or a succession of leaders, who claim to represent God's voice on earth and who claim authority greater than that of the Bible. The cultic teaching claims to be in harmony with the Bible but denies one or more of the cardinal doctrines presented therein.

Cults always derive from a 'parent' or 'host' religion.

Orville Swenson, in his book *The Perilous Path of Cultism*, suggests that a cult is "a religious group whose doctrines involve a distortion of biblical truth; whose dedication and subservience to their domineering leaders is frequently excessive and blind, and whose attitudes, aims, practices, and teachings are divisive, creating an exclusive body of deviates from historic biblical Christianity."

Cults Spring from Major Religions

While all these definitions are helpful and are also accurate to a degree, I think a key point they fail to include is that cults always derive from a "parent" or "host" religion. As [theology professor] Alan Gomes put it "cults grow out of and deviate from a previously established religion." Seen in this light, a cult *of Christianity*, according to Gomes, would be "a group of people, which claiming to be Christian, embraces a particular doctrinal system taught by an individual leader, group of leaders, or organization, which [system] denies (either explicitly or implicitly) one or more of the central doctrines of the Christian faith as taught in the sixty-six books of the Bible." Likewise, a cult *of Islam* would be, for example, the Nation of Islam, and a cult *of Hinduism* would be the Hare Krishnas. The Nation of Islam and the Hare Krishnas both derive from parent or host religions, yet both deviate from the doctrinal beliefs of these hosts. Hence they are "cults."

Gomes's definition is accurate, I believe, because it rightly recognizes that

1. Not every cult is a cult related to Christianity

2. Cults typically deviate from a host religion (whether Christianity, Islam, Hinduism, or some other religion)

3. Such cults can be headed by *individual leaders* (as is the case with the Unification Church, led by Reverend Moon) or by *an organization* (as is the case with the Jehovah's Witnesses, led by the Watchtower Society's Governing Body)

4. The point of deviation involves essential doctrines (for example, the deity of Christ) as opposed to mere peripheral doctrines (for example, the mode of baptism or style of church government)

5. Such deviations can be *explicit* (such as the Jehovah's Witnesses' flat denial of the Trinity) or *implicit* (for example, Mormons believe in the "heavenly Father" but redefine Him to be an exalted man)

A cult of Christianity claims to be Christian but in fact is not Christian because it explicitly or implicitly denies one or more central doctrines of the historic Christian faith.

Christian Doctrines and Cult Doctrines

If the above definition of a cult is correct, then we must also be clear concerning what constitutes the "major" or "essential" doctrines of Christianity. I believe there are five basic doctrines that are particularly pertinent for cultic studies:

1. *God* —including the biblical facts that there is *one* God who is *triune* in nature and is infinite and eternal

2. *Jesus Christ* —including the biblical facts that He is the second person of the Trinity and is therefore eternal God, was virgin born, died for humanity's sins, and was physically resurrected from the dead

3. *Mankind* —including the biblical facts that man was created in God's image, is forever distinct from God, is morally responsible to God, and is destined to live forever with God in heaven or to suffer eternally in hell, depending on whether he has been saved

4. *Sin and salvation* —including the biblical facts that all people are born into the world in a state of sin, that people can do nothing to merit their own salvation or earn favor with God, and that salvation is by grace alone through faith alone, based on the atonement wrought by Christ

5. *Scripture* —including the biblical facts that both the Old and New Testaments are inspired by God, are inerrant, and are therefore authoritative

A cult of Christianity, then, is a group that claims to be Christian but in fact is not Christian because it explicitly or implicitly denies one or more of these central doctrines of the historic Christian faith. . . .

Many cult leaders claim to have a direct pipeline to God. Mormon leader Brigham Young, for example, claimed, "I have had many revelations; I have seen and heard for myself; and know these things are true, and nobody on earth can disprove them." Reverend Moon of the Unification Church claimed to have received a revelation from Christ on Easter morning in 1936. Baha'is claim that the latest and greatest revelation from God has come through the prophet Baha'u'llah. Christian Scientists believe Mary Baker Eddy received revelations that are necessary to understand previous revelations in the Bible.

Cult Teachings Are Frequently Modified

It is interesting that the teachings of cults often change and that the groups need new "revelations" to justify such changes. Mormons once excluded African Americans from the priesthood. When social pressure was exerted on the Mormon church because of this racist practice, the Mormon president received a "new revelation" reversing the previous decree.

New revelations are certainly common within the New Age movement. New Age channelers claim to receive revelations from Ascended Masters. New Age psychics claim to be able to read the Akashic Record (an alleged cosmic energy field surrounding the earth that records all historic events). New Age astrologers derive their "revelations" from planetary alignments. Other New Agers engage in "automatic writing," wherein a person writes down information (including whole books) under the control of a spirit entity. (An example of this is *A Course in Miracles*, penned by Jewish psychologist Helen Schucman, who says a spirit named "Jesus" was the actual source of her words.)

In cults, greater credence is generally given to new revelations than past revelations (such as those found in the Bible). If there is ever a conflict between the new revelation and past revelations, the new revelation is always viewed as being authoritative.

When cults raise their own books or sets of books to the level of Scripture, 'God may now only speak as the sect deems proper. Thus the Word of God is brought under the yoke of man.'

In keeping with the above, many cults deny the sole authority of the Bible. Christian Scientists, for example, elevate

Mary Baker Eddy's book *Science and Health with Key to the Scriptures* to supreme authority. The Mormons say there are translational errors in the Bible and contend that *The Book of Mormon, Doctrine and Covenants,* and *The Pearl of Great Price* are more reliable than the Bible. New Agers place faith in such "holy books" as *The Aquarian Gospel of Jesus the Christ* and *A Course in Miracles.* Members of the Unification Church elevate Reverend Moon's *Divine Principle* to supreme authority. Scientologists believe the writings of [their founder] L. Ron Hubbard are "Scripture." The Jehovah's Witnesses' *Studies in the Scriptures* goes so far as to claim:

> If anyone lays the *Scripture Studies* aside, even after he has used them, after he has become familiar with them, after he has read them for 10 years—if he then lays them aside and ignores them and goes to the Bible alone, though he has understood his Bible for 10 years our experience shows that within two years he goes into darkness. On the other hand, if he had merely read the *Scripture Studies* with their references, and had not read a page of the Bible, as such, he would be in the light at the end of the two years, because he would have the light of the Scriptures.

Cults Try to Control Scripture

Cult expert Anthony Hoekema has cogently pointed out that when cults raise their own books or sets of books to the level of Scripture, "God is no longer allowed to speak as He does in the Bible; He may now speak only as the sect deems proper. Thus the Word of God is brought under the yoke of man." This is certainly the case with the Mormons, Jehovah's Witnesses, Christian Scientists, and some other other cults.

7

Anti-Cult Laws Are a Threat to Religious Freedom

Moira Shaw

Moira Shaw is deputy editor of the Sunday Examiner, *a Catholic weekly published in Hong Kong.*

"Anti-cult laws," which came to international attention after France passed one in 2001, are supposedly intended to prevent unscrupulous religious groups from manipulating their followers. Such laws are so subject to abuse, however, that they represent the greater danger. The main problem is that the broad language of anti-cult laws allows the definition of "cult" to include any belief system or program that influences people toward any practice or belief, with no call to judge such systems on their own merit. Hence, under such laws legitimate religious groups would become subject to severe restrictions, and their members' testimony be discounted as the programmed words of brainwashed victims. No government has the right to appoint itself sole judge of what constitutes a legitimate religion.

Millions of Catholics believe that during Mass, the priest turns ordinary bread and wine into the body and blood of Christ. Does this mean that Catholics are brainwashed flesh eaters and a danger to society? Have they been mentally manipulated and conned into believing in some hocus-pocus? Should the church be banned and its religious leaders locked up for interfering with the "psychology" of individuals?

Moira Shaw, "What Is a 'Cult'?" *Far Eastern Economic Review*, vol. 164, no. 29, July 26, 2001, p. 30. Republished with permission of *Far Eastern Economic Review*, conveyed through Copyright Clearance Center, Inc.

Rumours that Hong Kong was planning an anti-cult law similar to one in France [passed in May 2001] were dismissed by Chief Secretary Donald Tsang, a Catholic. His assurances followed a somewhat disturbing attempt by Chief Executive Tung Chee-hwa to pontificate on a religious matter. During a speech in the Legislative Council, Tung announced that the "Falun Gong [a movement which teaches mind-purification exercises] is not a religion" and that the debate about controlling what he calls an "evil cult" such as the Falun Gong was not "a question of religious freedom at all." Interestingly, by labelling the Falun Gong a "cult," but denying it the status of a "religion," Tung contradicted himself in his own language. The Chinese character for "cult" and "religion" is the same—*kao*. If a law on cults were introduced, would the word "cult" and "religion" be one and the same? Such is the inherent danger of toying with indefinable religious terms. [The main Chinese government does have anti-cult laws.]

Religion and Governments

While the United States draws a bold line between church and state, most countries have not made such a clear distinction between what belongs to God and what belongs to Caesar [the government]. Both regularly step on each other's toes. But when a state dabbles in the realm of religion, it can quickly become trapped in a maze of indefinable beliefs and arguments about freedom of individual thought. When states have sought to ban or control religious groups they have evoked sometimes violent passions as followers struggle to defend what they believe in. All hell breaks loose. Thus, few countries have chosen to pass laws regarding what their citizens may believe in or think; instead, laws have dealt mostly with a person's or group's actions. Freedom of thought is paramount.

France introduced its anti-cult law despite widespread opposition. The government says the bill is necessary to prevent and repress "cultic" movements that undermine human rights and fundamental freedoms. It has become a battle between freedoms.

"Cults" and "mind control" are indefinable categories without a precise scholarly or legal meaning. As such, any law dealing with these shadowy categories is clearly unenforceable. This is not to say that freedom of religion means anything goes, but the debate about what can be classified a religion is centuries old and embedded in a maze of personal opinions.

[The anti-cult law] enables private groups or the state to become involved in court cases against 'cults' on behalf of allegedly brainwashed victims.

The Dangers of Ambiguity

While the intention of the French law is clear and even admirable—it hopes to prevent individuals from being manipulated or abused—it is unclear what is meant by [its reference to] "prejudice to the personality" or even "psychological integrity." Sophisticated and subtle advertisements could be construed as manipulating the "psychological integrity" of viewers. Should ads be banned? France claims it has accepted international and domestic criticism and eliminated a specific offence [an earlier law] of mind control or brainwashing. But in fact the provision is still there, cosmetically disguised as an amendment to an existing section of the criminal code, now including "techniques likely to alter judgement." This is one of the most dangerous aspects of the law. It enables private groups or the state to become involved in court cases against "cults" on behalf of allegedly brainwashed victims. Even if the victims do not wish to entrust their representation to these associations, it can be argued that since they are brainwashed, their opinions don't count.

Fears of brainwashing aren't totally unfounded. Former members of some new religious movements have told horrifying stories of mental manipulation and physical abuse. Still, it is almost impossible to define what constitutes brainwashing. Moreover, in order to consider something as brainwashing, a judgement has to be made on whether the belief conveyed is right or wrong, otherwise it can be considered "teaching."

For France, its new anti-cult law may solve the problem caused by new religious movements. But it may also cause itself even more problems if it seeks to declare itself the sole judge of what is and is not a religion. Its citizens might simply refuse to believe it and accuse the state of brainwashing. Yet despite the dangers in the new law, those accused of breaking it can appeal to the European Court of Human Rights. But were Hong Kong to go this route, no similar fall-back would be available.

8

Anti-Cult Prejudice Denies Minority Religions a Fair Hearing

James R. Lewis

James R. Lewis is an associate lecturer in religious studies at the University of Wisconsin, Milwaukee. He is also the coeditor of Controversial New Religions *and author of* The Encyclopedia of Cults, Sects, and New Religions.

The "cult" label has hurt many a minority religious group's chances of a fair hearing. The word cult *alone conjures up a stereotype of a megalomaniac guru using innocent followers to feed his ego and carnal appetites, and psychological studies show that subjects are more likely to perceive a theoretical experience negatively if the story involves a recognized cult. In fact, however, many minority religions are benign and pose no threat to members or outsiders. Many people who help perpetuate the negative cult stereotype do so for personal gain—from the financial rewards of exit counseling to the personal rewards of winning a child-custody case.*

In the early 1970s, opposition to religious innovation was centered around deprogrammers—individuals who forcibly abducted members of nontraditional religions, locked them up in motel rooms, and assaulted their beliefs until they gave up their religious faith. Despite claims that deprogramming is a therapeutic intervention that breaks through cult members'

James R. Lewis, *Legitimating New Religions*. Piscataway, NJ: Rutgers University Press, 2003, pp. 198–213. Copyright © 2003 by James R. Lewis. Reprinted by permission of Rutgers University Press.

"hypnotic trance" and forces them to think again, it is clear that deprogrammers are little more than vigilantes acting at the behest of parents upset by the religious choices of their adult children. This negative evaluation of deprogramming is reinforced by the observation that, as a group, deprogrammers are largely uneducated individuals with little or no training in counseling.

Vested Interests of "Cult Watchdog Groups"

Deprogramming, controlled entirely by independent entrepreneurs, could never have developed into a viable profession without the simultaneous development of secular "cult watchdog groups." These organizations, despite vigorous public denials to the contrary, regularly referred concerned parents to deprogrammers. The evidence for this connection is overwhelming. For example, at the national gatherings of the Cult Awareness Network (CAN; formerly the Citizens Freedom Foundation, or CFF), one could always find a host of deprogrammers actively marketing their services to concerned parents in attendance. Deprogrammers, in turn, allegedly kicked back a certain percentage of their take to CAN. John Myles Sweeney, former national director of CAN/CFF, described this arrangement: "Because of the large amount of money they make due to referrals received from CFF members, deprogrammers usually kick back money to the CFF member who gave the referral. . . . The kick backs would either be in cash or would be hidden in the form of a tax-deductible 'donation' to the CFF." One of the results of the financial alliance between anti-cult groups and deprogrammers was that anti-cult groups acquired a vested interest in promoting the worst possible stereotypes of nontraditional religions. In other words, if one was profiting from referring worried parents to deprogrammers, it made no sense to inform parents that the religion their child had joined was comparatively benign. Instead, the tendency was to paint such religions in the exaggerated colors of fear and fanaticism, creating the anxiety that, unless their child was "rescued" immediately, he or she could end up as a lobotomized robot, suffering from permanent emotional and psychological damage.

Similarly, it made little sense to propagate a balanced view of alternative religions to the press. If one profited from the fear surrounding such groups, then it was natural to take every opportunity to repeat frightening rumors. It was, in fact, the two-decade-long interaction between the anti-cult movement and the media that has been responsible for the widespread view that all cults are dangerous organizations—this despite the fact that comparatively few such groups constitute a genuine threat, either to themselves or to society.

Public Prejudice Against Cults

However, with the exception of periodic attention from the mass media, the anti-cult movement (at least in North America) was and is relatively powerless. Even the influence that anti-cult spokespersons had in shaping public perceptions of cults was not based upon the intrinsic merit of their interpretations. Rather, anti-cultism feed [sic] upon—and in turn feed—a public *predisposition* to perceive nontraditional religions in a negative light. We might best understand this predisposition in terms of the social psychology of stereotyping. . . .

One of the more important cultural contradictions projected onto alternative religions is reflected in the brainwashing–mind control notion that is the core accusation leveled against such groups. Discourse that glorifies American society usually does so in terms of a rhetoric of liberty and freedom. However, while holding liberty as an ideal, we experience a social environment that is often quite restrictive. Most citizens work as employees in highly disciplined jobs where the only real freedom is the freedom to quit. Also, we are daily bombarded by advertising designed to influence our decisions and even to create new needs. Our frustration with these forms of influence and control is easily displaced and projected onto the separated societies of alternative religions, where the seemingly (but often not actually) restricted flow of information offers a distorted reflection of the situation we experience as members of the dominant society. . . .

Without this pre-existing disposition to construe nontraditional religions negatively, the anti-cult movement would have little or no social influence. However, even this influence is limited, in the sense that the stereotype the anti-cult movement has helped to shape has taken on a life of its own, independent of organized anti-cultism.

Once a stereotype is in place, a variety of different kinds of studies have shown that it becomes self-fulfilling and self-reinforcing.

In their role as moral entrepreneurs, anti-cult spokespersons have effectively marketed their negative stereotype of minority religions to the general public. Because of the pre-existing fit between this negative image and persistent social anxieties [related to the scapegoating of minorities], our society has overwhelmingly bought into the stereotype (or purchased the *moral commodity*, to [use] entrepreneurial metaphor). Because of widespread acceptance of the stereotype, the anti-cult movement could disappear tomorrow and anti-cult discourse would still continue to shape public perceptions of minority religions.

Testing Stereotypes

Once a stereotype is in place, a variety of different kinds of studies have shown that it becomes self-fulfilling and self-reinforcing. Thus in a [1998] study by [University of Minnesota psychologist Mark] Snyder, for example, students were asked to read a short biography about "Betty K," a fictitious woman. Her life story was constructed so that it would fulfill certain stereotypes of both heterosexuals and lesbians. In Snyder's words, "Betty, we wrote, never had a steady boyfriend in high school, but did go out on dates. And although we gave her a steady boyfriend in college, we specified that he was more of a close friend than anything else." A week later, they told some of the students that Betty was currently living with her husband and another group of students that she was living with another woman in a lesbian relationship. When subsequently requested to answer a series of questions about Betty, they found a marked tendency on the part of students to reconstruct her biography so as to conform to stereotypes about either heterosexuality or homosexuality, depending on the information they had received: "Those who believed that Betty was a lesbian remembered that Betty had never had a steady boyfriend in high school, but tended to neglect the fact that she had gone out on many dates in college. Those who believed that Betty was now a heterosexual, tended to remember that she had formed a steady relationship with a man in college, but tended to ignore the fact that this relationship was more of a friendship than a romance."

Minority religions lose their chance for a fair hearing as soon as the label 'cult' is successfully applied to them.

More directly relevant to the case at hand is an important article by [*Journal of Social Issues* editor] Jeffrey E. Pfeifer reporting the results of a similar study which compared responses to a biography in which a fictitious student, Bill, dropped out of college to enter a Catholic seminary, join the marines, or join the Moonies. The short biography incorporated elements of indoctrination often attributed to cults: "While at the facility, Bill is not allowed very much contact with his friends or family and he notices that he is seldom left alone. He also notices that he never seems to be able to talk to the other four people who signed up for the program and that he is continually surrounded by [Moonies, marines, priests] who make him feel guilty if he questions any of their actions or beliefs." When given a choice of describing Bill's indoctrination experience, subjects who thought Bill had joined the Catholic priesthood most often labeled his indoctrination "resocialization"; those who were told that he had joined the marines most frequently labeled the process "conversion"; and those who were under the impression that he had become a Moonie applied the label "brainwashing." On various other questions regarding the desirability and fairness of the indoctrination process, subjects who were told that Bill had joined the Moonies consistently evaluated his experience more negatively than subjects who were under the impression that Bill had joined either the marines or a priestly order.

The implication of this analysis is that minority religions lose their chance for a fair hearing as soon as the label "cult" is successfully applied to them. After that, the news media selectively seek out and present information that fits the stereotype. It is then only a matter of time before the group in question is completely "demonized."

Though the cult stereotype has come to dominate public discourse about minority religions, and though groups like the Unification Church [Moonies] and Peoples Temple [which committed mass suicide in 1978] seem to have become integral parts of that stereotype, there is enough ambiguity in the "cult" label to make its application in particular cases a matter of negotiation. Occasions for such negotiation arise in the context of social conflicts. For individuals or groups locked in certain kinds of struggles with members of minority religions, the cult stereotype represents a potent ideological resource which—if they are successful in swaying their immediate audience to reclassify a particular religion as a cult—marshals opinion against their opponent, potentially tipping the balance of power in their favor.

The Cult Stereotype as a Weapon

Situations in which this strategy can work are not restricted to the kinds of conflicts that are picked up by the national news media. For example, the stigma of the cult stereotype has been effectively deployed in child custody cases, in which one parent's membership in a minority religion is portrayed as indicative of her or his unworthiness as a parent. For such limited-domain legal conflicts, however, it is difficult to deploy the stereotype unless there is some larger, earlier conflict that led to press coverage in which the particular minority religion in question was labeled a cult. Lacking earlier bad press, the cult label can still sometimes be made to stick on the basis of testimony by disgruntled former members.

For the most part, individuals involved in such relatively limited conflicts do not become full-time anti-cult crusaders. Although they may enter into a relationship with the anti-cult movement, they normally drift away from this involvement within a short time after the termination of their particular struggle. To refer back to the entrepreneurial model, these people are not so much moral entrepreneurs as they are consumers of a moral commodity—they have "purchased" a pre-packaged cult stereotype and brought it to bear as one tool in the array of resources they have assembled to legitimate their cause. They may, of course, still have to exercise persuasive skills in getting the public or the court to accept the applicability of the stereotype, but otherwise they are not invested in the product per se. If anti-cult rhetoric fails to accomplish their end, but some other tool works in their particular conflict, they are usually quite ready to dispose of the cult stereotype and adopt an entirely different angle of attack.

As a low-intensity group that does not make excessive demands upon either the time or the resources of most participants, MSIA [the Movement of Spiritual Inner Awareness, a "soul transcendence" group] was largely overlooked by the anti-cult movement until the late 1980s. In 1988, the *Los An-*

geles Times published a highly critical article on MSIA. A similar article then appeared in *People* magazine. Both pieces dwelt on charges by ex-staff members that MSIA's founder, John-Roger Hinkins, had sexually exploited them. Depending significantly upon the testimony of disgruntled ex-staff and drawing heavily on the cult stereotype, MSIA was portrayed as an organization that was created for no other purpose than to serve the financial, sexual, and ego needs of John-Roger Hinkins. . . .

In at least one case, a parent's association with [a so-called cult] was effectively used against her by the other parent in a dispute involving their mutual offspring.

Use of Cult Stereotypes for Selfish Ends

In the words of Michael Homer, an expert in legal cases involving minority religions, "Religious practices and beliefs have also become the subject of child custody cases where nonmembers attempt to highlight nontraditional aspects of a spouse's or ex-spouse's religion to obtain custody of a minor child. Nonmembers seek to show that the religion deviates from social normalcy and, therefore, adversely affects the child's behavior. It is argued that the church's influence is mentally, physically, and emotionally detrimental to the child's well-being. Nonmembers have been successful when the court determines that the practices complained of are not merely religious but are detrimental practices that harm the child." In at least one case, a parent's association with MSIA was effectively used against her by the other parent in a dispute involving their mutual offspring. In this particular case, a divorced mother petitioned the court to permit her to relocate in order to take a position in an MSIA-inspired organization offering human potentials seminars. As his primary strategy for delegitimating his wife's position, the ex-husband argued that he did not want his son involved in a cult. To support his contention, he dragged up all of the old rumors about John-Roger and MSIA in an effort to prevent his ex-wife from leaving the state. Perceiving that not only would she have a difficult time winning, but also that her husband might undertake further actions that could result in her son being taken from her, she dropped her petition.

What is especially ironic about this case is that for several decades the father was deeply involved in EST [Erhard Seminar Training]—a human potentials group that has *very* frequently (*far more* frequently than MSIA) been labeled a cult. As someone whose participation in EST has likely sensitized him to the cult controversy, the ex-husband's utilization of the stereotype was clearly little more than a tactic intended to win support for his side of the case, rather than a reflection of deeply held views about the dangers of sinister cults. As the mother stated in a telephone interview, she felt that her former spouse was advised, "Shoot her where you think you can hurt her," and that her involvement in a MSIA-related organization was simply a convenient target.

The chances of this man becoming a full-time anti-cult crusader are practically nil. Here, . . . it is clear that the cult stereotype is an ideological resource, deployed without a deep investment in the stereotype per se. This way of understanding the cult image's role in particular struggles represents a variation on earlier theorizing. Most recent theorizing has focused on the anti-cult movement's campaign to win acceptance of both its ideology and its agenda by the greater society. By shifting the point of focus from this broad level to more particular struggles, we are able to see that, in the context of grassroots conflicts, the cult stereotype becomes a moral commodity—an ideological resource that can easily be set aside if it is not persuasive or if some other tactic better suits the situation.

9

Cults Foster Us-Versus-Them Attitudes

Arthur J. Deikman

Arthur J. Deikman, a clinical professor of psychiatry at the University of California, San Francisco, is recognized as an expert on cult psychology. He is author of The Wrong Way Home: Uncovering the Patterns of Cult Behavior in American Society.

The biggest threats posed by cults are based on "us versus them" attitudes. Nearly all such groups see outsiders as evil, dangerous, of the devil, less than human. This cult mentality is a threat however it is expressed: by the mainstream religious leader who opposes interfaith services for fear of implying all religions are equal; by the everyday citizen who calls brutal violence terrorism when They do it to Us, but not when Our people do exactly the same thing to Them; by the politician who refuses to acknowledge that any *foreign hatred of his government may be partly justified; and by the newspaper that gives extensive coverage to the violent acts of certain groups while ignoring similar behavior in others. All such attitudes help create a picture of the "outsider" as less human and undermine efforts toward equality and peaceful coexistence.*

[T]he quickest tip-off that something is amiss occurs when you see members of a group devalue outsiders while ignoring the faults of the leader and fellow believers. Outsiders—Them—are identified as inferior, bad, or damned.

Arthur J. Deikman, *Them and Us: Cult Thinking and the Terrorist Threat*. Berkeley, CA: Bay Tree Publishing, 2003, pp. 170–86. Copyright © 2003 Arthur J. Deikman. Reproduced by permission.

Those in the cult group—Us—are perceived as superior, good, or saved. We see this in its most extreme form in the mind of the terrorist.

Yet to think this way is to distort reality, for, in fact, human beings are not fundamentally different from each other. We know that when barriers are reduced or set aside, people see themselves in the Other. Indeed . . . as I listened to people recounting their cult histories . . . they made me aware of the ubiquitous, everyday presence of cult behavior in people like myself who were not members of full-blown cults. Psychologically speaking, the abiding wish for security and protection makes the human race one family. Cult thinking says the opposite. . . .

The attraction of a fantasy of ultimate salvation was seen in the guru cults that flourished in the United States in the 1960s and 1970s. . . . Large numbers of disciples looked to "enlightened" masters who could provide answers that would give their lives direction and meaning, culminating in union with divine purpose. Some went on to make headlines via their own version of martyrdom. The [mass suicides of the] Branch Davidians at Waco, Texas, led by David Koresh [1993] and the Peoples Temple at Jonestown, Guyana, led by Jim Jones [1978], were lurid examples of violence turned against the members at the behest of religious leaders. Members of the Aum cult in Japan released poison gas in the Tokyo subway [in 1995] as part of a strategy of killing all outsiders to prepare the world for a new order.

Terrorism in the Eye of the Beholder

A striking example of Them-and-Us psychology call be seen in the fact that the perception of what constitutes an act of terror depends on who is doing it. Some idea of this cult-like selective vision can be gained by considering a poll conducted among Palestinians in December 2001. As reported by Gail Luft in *Foreign Affairs* magazine:

> More than 94 percent of Palestinians told pollsters that they viewed Israeli incursions into Area A as acts of terror, while 82 percent refused to characterize the killing of 21 Israeli youths outside Tel Aviv disco six months earlier [June 2001] that way.... only 41 percent of Palestinians ... viewed the September 11 attacks as terrorism. And 94 percent reported that they would characterize a hypothetical Israeli use of chemical or biological weapons against Palestinians as terrorism, whereas only 26 percent would say the same about Palestinian use of those weapons against Israel. . . .

It is important that we all become aware how cult thinking affects our responses. The cost of unrecognized cult thinking is apparent in the case of the U.S. government's refusal to recognize the connection between the extreme behavior of cults, such as the Branch Davidians of Waco, Texas, and the less obvious cult tendencies of our own familiar religions. The FBI devalued the Davidians as if it were a criminal organization—not as a religious group with a leader worshipped by disciples. Had the FBI been more willing to label the group a religion, albeit one with a self-righteously grandiose leader, it might have sought out an appropriate religious leader to talk with David Koresh and work out a religion-based rationale for a solution that didn't end in the group's immolation. Instead, it employed an assault team to "rescue" the "hostages" [leading to the incineration of the Davidians' compound with 76 fatalities]. I suspect this reluctance to categorize the Branch Davidians as a religious group also may have prevented the FBI from seeing that Koresh would never submit to an inglorious conclusion to his story and that his followers would obey him even to the point of losing their own lives.

The Cult Mindset in Mainstream Groups

At the time, national media displayed a similar reluctance to draw parallels between the Branch Davidians and mainstream groups. During the Waco siege and its aftermath, I was interviewed a number of times by news programs as an expert on cult psychology. On two of those occasions, I pointed out that the behavior of some anti-abortion groups in harassing patients and staff of abortion clinics—which culminated in murders of staff and numerous bombings of clinics—reflected cult thinking not fundamentally different than what had taken place among the Davidians. These comments were edited out and did not appear during the broadcasts of the interviews. Indeed, many people even today would be hesitant to call the perpetrators of "pro-life" violence terrorists, though similar thinking is promoted by [the terrorist organization] al Qaeda with much the same religious fervor.

Being able to recognize cult thinking at work in our own backyard is becoming increasingly important. Fundamentalist groups that devalue the outsider and avoid or punish dissent are on the rise all over the world. Yet despite the fact that the worst violence against human beings has been committed by self-righteous people citing God as their authority—al Qaeda being perhaps one of the most remarkable examples—we avoid scrutinizing followers of religions in our own backyard with the same critical eye we cast on those whose religious form is in some way alien.

Consider a news report by Alan Cooperman for the *Washington Post* in July of 2002:

> A high-ranking Lutheran pastor has been suspended from his duties and ordered to apologize to all Christians for participating with Muslims, Jews, Sikhs, and Hindus in an interfaith prayer service in Yankee Stadium after September 11. The Missouri Synod's national second vice president, Reverend Wallace Schultz wrote in the suspension letter: '. . . a crystal clear signal was given to others watching the event and to [cable broadcaster] C-Span. The signal was: While there may be differences as to how people worship or pray, in the end, all religions pray to the same God. . . . To participate with pagans in an interfaith service and, addition-

ally, to give the impression that there might be more than one God, is an extremely serious offence against the God of the Bible.'

Notice that "pagans" is used to categorize Muslims, Jews, Sikhs, and Hindus. From the point of view of the Reverend Schultz, they are clearly the Outsider and of lesser value....

Them is the enemy, so they cannot be Good, as we are.
The irony is that we are all Them to someone else.

Cult Thinking and the Desire for Security

Cult thinking is basic to all human beings because of our childhood dependence on parents. Although later as adults we have at our disposal much more sophisticated mental capacities, we carry with us a heritage of dependency: the vision and hope for a super family providing the security of the back seat of the car. This longing . . . can lead to terribly destructive results beginning with the perception of other humans as Them. Them is the enemy, so they cannot be Good, as we are. We blame Them, hate Them, exploit Them, and kill Them. The irony is that we are all Them to someone else. Currently, we are Them to al Qaeda, and They want to kill Us. Can we be realistic in our response to this threat? Can we avoid devaluing al Qaeda as they do us, selecting facts to support our own fantasy of being Good, unlike Them? A more realistic view may seem to offer less security than does fantasy, but actually it offers more. If we allow ourselves to see our own fantasies, we too can exit from cult thinking and respond to terrorism more effectively.

From a larger perspective, it may be that our struggle to deal with the terrorist threat could make clear the danger inherent in any ideology, any system of belief offering utopian goals at the cost of compliance, conformity, and the suppression of dissent. The warning sign of ideology is the sharp division between Them and Us, whether it is based on politics, economics, race or religion. The possibilities for destruction and misery endemic to such beliefs have been multiplied many times by modern science. As a result, the few can now destroy the many, and that power is becoming increasingly accessible. I hope the danger may cause us to recognize that we all share the same needs for meaning, security, and a positive future. From that point of view we are one family. Understanding this fundamental fact is the antidote to cult thinking.

There is no Them. There is only Us.

10

The Threat of a Cult Depends on the Observer's Worldview

Eugene V. Gallagher

Eugene V. Gallagher is the Rosemary Park Professor of Religious Studies at Connecticut College in New London. His extensive writings on religious movements include the books Expectation and Experience: Explaining Religious Conversion *and* The New Religious Movements Experience in America; *he is also coauthor (with James D. Tabor) of* Why Waco? Cults and the Battle for Religious Freedom in America.

New religious movements, or "cults," are regularly subjected to accusations of megalomania, lack of scruples, and inherently illogical beliefs. The trouble with many such indictments is that they are based on vague or unjustified assumptions. Cult critics regularly fail to distinguish between deep religious conviction and mental imbalance, psychopathic leaders and cult leaders in general, extreme and acceptable religious claims, conversion and coercive persuasion, or objective researchers and cult apologists. Likewise, most cult opponents claim to be advocates of objective truth whose only interest is fighting extreme worldviews and behavior, but they regularly fail to see how their own worldviews color their assumptions and behavior. Every worldview, common or extreme, makes obvious sense to those who hold it. With a commitment to academic objectivity and an awareness of one's limitations, however, it should be possible to make a fair and reasonably unbiased study of religious groups one disagrees with.

At least some indictments of cults raise the question of whether personal submission to the will of a deity, either directly or as mediated by a human leader, must necessarily be taken as an indication of pathology. [Psychologist Sigmund] Freud, for example, famously argued in *The Future of an Illusion* that religious ideas are merely wish-fulfillments that should be left behind as the individual achieves a progressively more accurate and mature grasp of reality. Since religions frequently include traffic with supernatural entities whose existence cannot be scientifically confirmed, they are all vulnerable to criticisms that they intentionally mislead their followers. Since any lasting religious group features some kind of leadership, they also could be open to the criticisms that they fail to provide full disclosure to prospective members, act in their own self-interest, and devote their energies to keeping members enmeshed in a wholly fictional world. It is possible, then, to conceive of many anticult activists as either implicit or explicit proponents of a contemporary secular worldview that is fundamentally at odds with any religious claims, whether they come from established or new religious movements.

The adversaries of cults often try emphasizing that they deal with observable behavior rather than theological ideas. But behavior is not unmotivated.

Cult Opponents Are Not as Objective as They Claim

Contemporary cult opponents' claims to be selfless servants of objective truth are embedded in a particular view of the world as much as are the Raëlians' belief in a race of space creatures known as Elohim or The Family's expectation of the imminent end of the world. As a result, the conflict between new religious movements and their adversaries is more complicated than it may superficially appear. Both sides are deeply committed to specific views of the world, history, human nature, and the goals of life. Each side accepts a certain set of fundamental conceptions as rock-bottom givens. In many ways the worldviews of the secular antagonists are as incompatible with those of new religious movements as are the worldviews of their Christian or Jewish foes. At bottom, the different groups espouse fundamentally different values. For example, in the eyes of many religious people the drive for individual self-determination will eventually come into conflict with the necessity of obedience to the will of God. More specifically, for observant Jews obedience to the whole Torah of Moses militates against acknowledging Jesus of Nazareth as the Messiah, and the Church of Jesus Christ of Latter-day Saints' acceptance of the *Book of Mormon* as "another testament of Jesus Christ" strikes many Christians as heretical. Consequently, the assertion that one worldview is obviously more correct, true, or somehow simply better than another demands a complex and detailed supporting argument; the truth of the assertion is never self-evident. In most cases, however, cultural opponents of cults have been much better at describing what they are against than what they are for.

Theology Influences Practice

The adversaries of cults often try to minimize the role that worldviews play in the ongoing cultural conflict by emphasizing that they deal with observable behavior rather than theological ideas. But behavior is not unmotivated, and many theological ideas are specifically intended to inspire distinctive types of behavior. The expectation of the imminent end of the world, for example, is a theological idea, but in the cases of both the Branch Davidians and the Children of God/The Family it motivated communal living arrangements, sustained missionary activity, and promoted the acceptance of the paramount authority of David Koresh and Moses David Berg, respectively. Scholars of religion have long noted the mutual reinforcement of ideas and actions. One of the founding fathers of the sociology of religion, Emile Durkheim, defined religion as a set of beliefs and practices that unites all who adhere to them into a single moral community. Similarly [anthropologist] Clifford Geertz proposed that religions form both moods and motivations, both states of mind and feeling and tendencies to act. Thus, when anticultists sever thought from action they destroy the coherence of religious systems. Actions only become meaningful within a coherent intellectual framework or worldview. The act of touching one's head to the ground, for example, could be viewed as either appropriate respect or craven cowardice, depending on the context of interpretation provided by a particular worldview. What cult foes do by ignoring the theological motivation or rationale for certain actions is simply to substitute a motivation that the cult members themselves would not recognize or countenance for one that the members would acknowledge and endorse. In the end, the anticultists' argument boils down to the confident assertion that they know better than any cult members what their behavior really means.

The anticultists [fail to see] the interactions of leaders and followers; followers are simply acted upon and leaders retain unshakeable command and control.

The "Deranged Cult Leader" Stereotype

Cult opponents also adopt an unwavering focus on the leader. In [psychologist] Margaret Singer's words, "a cult is a mirror of what is inside the cult leader." When Singer looks at cults she sees the monstrous pathology of Jim Jones played out over and over again. In her view "all cults are variations on a single theme." If that is indeed the case, the pathological aspects of one case can be expected to reappear in another. Rather than making a statistical survey of however many cult movements she might identify in the contemporary United States, Singer instead chooses to advance a few dramatic cases, most notably [those involving the mass death at] Jonestown and Waco, as accurate models of all others. What is true about one is implicitly avowed to be true about all others. The leader, who in anticult rhetoric is inherently deranged, unstable, manipulative, and corrupt, is the pivot around which the entire anticult movement turns. It is remarkable, then, that in anticult literature there is little serious engagement with either classic or contemporary analyses of leadership. Although the term *charisma* is frequently mentioned, there appears to be little understanding of how and in what context sociologist Max Weber developed the term for the analysis of leadership nor of the subsequent academic discussions of how charismatic leadership is claimed, recognized, denied, challenged, and adapted in specific social contexts. [Activist] Steven Hassan, for example, observes that "charismatic cult leaders often make extreme claims of divine or 'otherworldly' power to exercise influence over their members." Hassan does not disclose, however, what makes a claim extreme as opposed to average, the bases on which power is asserted to be divine or otherworldly, the criteria against which an audience measures such claims to see whether they are persuasive, the specific channels through which such claims become influential, the degree to which they exercise influence on different members of an audience, or the duration of their purported influence. In the stereotype promulgated by cult adversaries the characteristics of the cult leader are unvarying, influence flows only from the leader to the followers, and the same exploitative relationship is repeated over and over again. The anticultists see little if any dynamism in the interactions of leaders and followers; followers are simply acted upon and leaders retain unshakeable command and control. In their view, the situation is the same in Heaven's Gate as it was in the Peoples Temple and as it was at the origins of the Mormon church. If a group is defined as a cult, everything else necessarily follows. Historians, sociologists, and scholars of religion, however, have developed rather different understandings of leadership.

Choosing a Descriptive and Analytical Vocabulary

As the brief review of contemporary cult controversies shows, there is substantial variation and instability in fundamental descriptive terms. Members of both the anticult and countercult movements have wrenched the term *cult* from its previously stable academic meanings and turned it into a polemical weapon. Sociologists and historians of religion have tried to establish the terms *new religious movement, alternative religion, emergent religion,* or even *first-generation religion* as relatively neutral descriptions of sectarian and other innovative groups, only to be accused of being cult apologists when they fail to view the objects of their study with sufficient alarm. Similarly, cult opponents believe that intentionally neutral terms like *conversion* are pallid substitutes that thoroughly misread the power dynamics in what they see as coercive persuasion, mind control, or brainwashing. Inevitably, to choose a descriptive vocabulary is to take a stand in the cult wars that show few signs of abating. . . . This [author] will employ the general descriptive term *new religious movement,* with the implicit conviction that it *does not* constitute an endorsement of any particular group or class of groups. It simply follows the important analytical distinction between description and explanation. With specific reference to the topic of religious experience, Wayne Proudfoot has argued that a student of religion's first responsibility is to render the experience as clearly as possible in terms that the subject of the experience can acknowledge as substantially accurate. As Proudfoot writes, "where it is the subject's experience which is the object of study, that experience must be identified under a description that can plausibly be attributed to him." That description, however, does not commit the observer to the explanation of that experience that the subject himself or herself would hold. Again, in Proudfoot's terms, "the explanation the analyst offers of that same experience is another matter altogether. It need not be couched in terms familiar or acceptable to the subject. It must be an explanation of the experience as identified under the subject's description, but the subject's approval of the explanation is not required."

Each new religious group has both explicit and implicit claims for its own significance that make ultimate sense within its own view of the world.

Description and Interpretation of Religious Movements

Description and interpretation or explanation of religious experience are two separate, if overlapping, intellectual processes. The same holds true for new religious movements. Religious groups that their opponents see as heresies or as destructive cults see themselves as religions, and new groups often emphasize their innovative nature. It is thus descriptively accurate to describe a group like the Church Universal and Triumphant (CUT), the Unification Church, the Rastafarians, or the International Society for Krishna Consciousness as both new and religious, insofar as that accords with their self-understanding. That does not, however, also entail accepting assertions that CUT has accurately recovered the lost teachings of Jesus, that the Unificationists have identified the Lord of the Second Advent, that smoking marijuana (*ganja*) is a sacrament, or that the Bhagavad-Gita should become the sole scripture for all humanity. Each new religious group has both explicit and implicit claims for its own significance that make ultimate sense within its own view of the world. Outside observers, however, as Proudfoot emphasizes, need not accept any religion's claims about itself and may certainly choose to offer other analytical and interpretative contexts for the data they use. The adoption of the term *new religious movement* does not, therefore, represent a substantial ideological claim about the ideas and practices of any specific group or about new religious movements in general. But that choice of a descriptive term does express the critical opinion that new religious movements can be studied in the same ways and for the same purposes that any other religious phenomena are studied, because that study can yield interesting, significant, and even helpful insight into how human beings construct meaningful lives. As such, the general orientation of this [writing] does represent a commitment to the standards of argument and evidence that typify the academic study of religion, particularly as it is practiced in North American colleges and universities. Anyone who enters the discussion of cults or new religious movements—students, teachers, reporters and commentators in the media, interested persons in the general public, members or partisans of particular groups, or their dedicated antagonists—unavoidably stakes a claim by the choice of a descriptive vocabulary and the implicit endorsement of the interpretive framework that it is founded on. In a contentious atmosphere, one can only hope to express one's position with clarity and precision, but one cannot control how others perceive it. It is in the best interests of everyone if those claims are clearly articulated, explicitly supported with accessible evidence, and directly related to their fundamental authorizing assumptions.

Organizations to Contact

American Academy of Religion (AAR)
825 Houston Mill Rd. NE, Ste. 300, Atlanta, GA   30329-4205
(404) 727-3049 • fax: (404) 727-7959
e-mail: aar@aarweb.org
Web site: www.aarweb.org

AAR is an association of academic professionals dedicated to "fostering excellence in the study of religion." Founded in 1909, the academy publishes *Journal of the AAR, Religious Studies News,* and numerous other books and periodicals. Archives of articles (some accessible only to members) and press releases can be found on the Web site.

Center for Studies on New Religions (CESNUR)
PO Box 90709, Santa Barbara, CA   93190-0709
805-967-7721 • fax: (805) 683-4876
e-mail: jgordon@linkline.com
Web site: www.cesnur.org

CESNUR is an international network of scholarly associations working in the field of new religious movements; the main headquarters is in Torino, Italy. Established in 1988, the network is dedicated to providing accurate information about various esoteric and spiritual movements, and to countering propaganda from both cults and anticult groups. CESNUR also guides former cult members to helpful resources. The Web site (published in Italian with English translations available for most sections) offers numerous resource lists, including the center's library catalog of over twenty thousand volumes. Topics range from the New Age to mainstream religion to occult-related popular culture.

Church of Scientology International
6331 Hollywood Blvd., Suite 1200, Los Angeles, CA   90028
(323) 960-3500 • fax: (323) 960-3508
e-mail: mediarelationsdir@scientology.net
Web site: www.scientology.org

Scientology, which adherents take to mean "the study of truth" or "knowing how to know," was founded by science fiction writer L. Ron Hubbard; the church was established in California in 1954 and officially recognized by the IRS as a non-profit, tax-exempt religious organization in 1993. The church preaches a doctrine of self-realization and enlightenment through spiritual awareness, and describes itself as the only major new world religion of the twentieth century. The Web site explains Scientology's history and beliefs in detail, debates its critics, and provides information on its worldwide evangelical and social service activities.

Cult Awareness Network (CAN)
PO Box 2265, Bonita Springs, FL   34133
1-800-556-3055
e-mail: can@cultawarenessnetwork.org
Web site: http://www.cultawarenessnetwork.org/

The "new" Cult Awareness Network is an organization owned by associates of the Church of Scientology dedicated to distributing information on religious movements and promoting peaceful religious debate. The original CAN was founded in 1974 as the Citizens Freedom Foundation, dedicated to educating the public on alleged cult brainwashing and to helping former cult members readjust to society. The organization adopted the name Cult Awareness Network in 1986, but its involvement in deprogramming and other controversial practices brought about a series of lawsuits (many initiated by the Church of Scientology) that caused it to declare bankruptcy ten years later; the current owners subsequently bought its assets at auction. The current CAN Web site provides numerous articles and links to information on various religions, as well as criticism of the old CAN and other cult opponents.

CultsOnCampus.com
PO Box 11011, Carson, CA   90749
(310) 283-2888
e-mail: cultsoncampus@cultsoncampus.com
Web site: www.cultsoncampus.com

CultsOnCampus is dedicated to countering the recruiting tactics of cults seeking new members among college students. Much of the organization's work focuses on the International Church of Christ (ICOC); not to be confused with the Christian denominations known as the Church of Christ or the United Church of Christ, the ICOC preaches an exclusivist and ultraconservative version of Christianity. The Web site provides a resource list and links to various news archives.

Hartford Institute for Religion Research
Hartford Seminary, Hartford, CT   06105-2260
(860) 509-9543 • fax: (860) 509-9551
e-mail: hirr@hartsem.edu
Web site: http://hirr.hartsem.edu/

The Hartford Institute for Religion Research is "committed to providing quality . . . scientific religion research information that is helpful for religious leaders and the general public." Its Web site includes a section on new religious movements with links to relevant sites and an extensive collection of articles.

Information Network Focus on
Religious Movements (INFORM)
Houghton Street, London   WC2A 2AE
   UK
+44 20 7955 7654 • fax: +44 20 7955 7679
e-mail: inform@lse.ac.uk
Web site: www.inform.ac/infmain.html

INFORM is an independent charity founded in 1988 and based at the London School of Economics. Its purpose is to provide objective and accurate information on new and alternative religious movements. The Web site provides a "Concern/

Fact" evaluation page regarding the typical cult experience, plus a calendar of events and guidelines for friends and families of new converts.

International Cultic Studies Association (ICSA)

PO Box 2265, Bonita Springs, FL   34133
(239) 514-3081 • fax: (305) 393-8193
e-mail: aff@affcultinfoserve.com
Web site: www.csj.org

The ICSA is an interdisciplinary network of academicians, former cult members, and other interested parties dedicated to educating the public on authoritarian tactics and zealotry as expressed in alternative religious movements and similar groups. Founded in 1979 as AFF (American Family Foundation), ICSA adopted its current name in 2004 as better suiting an increasingly international and scholarly focus. Today it is the leading professional organization in its field. The Web site provides access to archives of the association's journal, *Cultic Studies Review*, along with an online bookstore, information service, and calendar of events.

Ontario Consultants on Religious Tolerance (OCRT)

PO Box 128, Watertown, NY   13601-0128
fax: (613) 547-9015
e-mail: ocrt@religioustolerance.org
Web site: www.religioustolerance.org

The OCRT is a Canada-based agency dedicated to promoting individual religious freedom by distributing accurate information, debating false information, and discussing hot topics in current religious debate. The organization strives to present information from as many points of view as possible. Its Web site presents essays on numerous religions and other topics, along with a discussion forum and a list of recommended reading.

Reasoning from the Scriptures Ministries

PO Box 2526, Frisco, TX   75034
(214) 618-0912 • fax: (214) 853-4370
e-mail: ronrhodes@earthlink.net
Web site: www.ronrhodes.org

Reasoning from the Scriptures is a Christian ministry dedicated to countering the claims of cults and other non-Christian religions through apologetic debate. The ministry puts out a bimonthly e-publication called *Reasoning from the Scriptures Newsletter*, with subscriptions available through the Web site. The site also features an online bookstore and a large library of links to related Web content.

Rick A. Ross Institute of New Jersey

Newport Financial Center, Jersey City, NJ   07310-1756
(201) 434-9234 • fax: (201) 435-7108
e-mail: info@rickross.com
Web site: www.rickross.com

The Rick A. Ross Institute is a nonprofit organization dedicated to research and public education on the topic of "destructive cults" and controversial religious movements. The Web site provides extensive resources and links for researchers, former cult members, and the public; an Open Forum page is included.

Steven Alan Hassan's Freedom of Mind Center

PO Box 45223, Somerville, MA   02145
(617) 628-9918 • fax: (617) 628-8153
e-mail: center@freedomofmind.com
Web site: www.freedomofmind.com

The Freedom of Mind Center, operated by anticult activist and counselor Steven Hassan, is dedicated to "combating cult mind control" (the title of Hassan's best-known book) and easing former cult members' readjustment to mainstream society. The center is also dedicated to educating the public on the dangers of cults; the Web site provides a lengthy recommended reading list as well as numerous other resources for former cult members and the general public.

Watchman Fellowship
913 Huffman Rd., Birmingham, AL   35215
(205) 833-2858 • fax: (205) 833-8699
Web site: www.watchman.org

Watchman Fellowship is "a ministry of Christian discernment" dedicated to evaluating new religious movements and the occult from a Christian perspective. Founded in 1979, the organization now has several offices in the United States and eastern Europe. The Web site features a "Programs and Presentations" page, a library of articles, and links to current national and international religious news stories.

Bibliography

Books

David V. Barrett	*The New Believers: Sects, "Cults," and Alternative Religions.* New York: Cassell, 2003.
Helen A. Berger, ed.	*Witchcraft and Magic: Contemporary North America.* Philadelphia: University of Pennsylvania Press, 2005.
Brenda E. Brasher	*Give Me That Online Religion.* Piscataway, NJ: Rutgers University Press, 2004.
David G. Bromley and J. Gordon Melton, eds.	*Cults, Religion, and Violence.* Cambridge, England: Cambridge University Press, 2002.
Peter Clarke	*Encyclopedia of New Religious Movements.* Oxford, England: Routledge, 2005.
Douglas E. Cowan	*Bearing False Witness?: An Introduction to the Christian Countercult.* Westport, CT: Praeger, 2003.
Dereck Daschke and W. Michael Ashcraft, eds.	*New Religious Movements: A Documentary Reader.* New York: New York University Press, 2005.
Derek H. Davis and Barry Hankins, eds.	*New Religious Movements and Religious Liberty in America.* Waco, TX: Baylor University Press, 2003.

L.L. Dawson

Cults and New Religious Movements. Oxford, England: Blackwell, 2003.

Arthur J. Deikman

Them and Us: Cult Thinking and the Terrorist Threat. Berkeley, CA: Bay Tree, 2003.

Amy Johnson Frykholm

Rapture Culture: Left Behind in Evangelical America. New York: Oxford University Press, 2004.

Eugene V. Gallagher

The New Religious Movements Experience in America. Westport, CT: Greenwood, 2004.

Janja Lalich

Bounded Choice: True Believers and Charismatic Cults. Berkeley and Los Angeles: University of California Press, 2004.

James R. Lewis

Legitimating New Religions. New Brunswick, NJ: Rutgers University Press, 2003.

James R. Lewis

Oxford Handbook of New Religious Movements. New York: Oxford University Press, 2003.

James R. Lewis and Jesper Aagaard Petersen, eds.

Controversial New Religions. Oxford, England: Oxford University Press, 2005.

Phillip Charles Lucas and Thomas Robbins, eds.

New Religious Movements in the Twenty-First Century: Legal, Political, and Social Challenges in Global Perspective. New York: Routledge, 2004.

Claire Mason
New Religious Movements: The Impact on Our Lives. London: Hodder Children's Books, 2003.

Carol S. Matthews
New Religions. Philadelphia: Chelsea House, 2005.

Sean McCloud
Making the American Religious Fringe: Exotics, Subversives & Journalists, 1955–1993. Chapel Hill: University of North Carolina Press, 2004.

Susan J. Palmer
Aliens Adored: Rael's UFO Religion. Piscataway, NJ: Rutgers University Press, 2004.

Christopher Partridge, ed.
Dictionary of Contemporary Religion in the Western World. Downer's Grove, IL: Inter-Varsity, 2001.

Joanne Pearson, ed.
Belief Beyond Boundaries: Wicca, Celtic Spirituality, and the New Age. Burlington, VT: Ashgate, 2002.

Ron Rhodes
The Challenge of the Cults and New Religions. Grand Rapids, MI: Zondervan, 2001.

James T. Richardson, ed.
Regulating Religion: Case Studies from Around the Globe. New York: Springer, 2003.

John A. Saliba
Understanding New Religious Movements. Oxford, England: AltaMira, 2003.

Margaret Thaler Singer
Cults in Our Midst: The Continuing Fight Against Their Hidden Menace. San Francisco: Jossey-Bass, 2003.

Robert L. Snow   *Deadly Cults: The Crimes of True Believers.* Westport, CT: Praeger, 2003.

Benjamin
Zablocki and
Thomas Robbins,
eds.   *Misunderstanding Cults: Searching for Objectivity in a Controversial Field.* Toronto: University of Toronto Press, 2001.

Periodicals

Rob Boston   "Breaking the Opus Dei Code," *Church & State*, May 2006.

Joseph E. Davis   "Victim Memories and Victim Selves: False Memory Syndrome and the Power of Accounts," *Social Problems*, November 2005.

Robert F. Drinan   "A Victory for Religious Freedom," *National Catholic Reporter*, March 31, 2006.

T.B. Dykeman   "The Rhetoric of Religious 'Cults': Terms of Use and Abuse," *Choice*, April 2006.

Bryan Edelman
and James T.
Richardson   "Imposed Limitations on Freedom of Religion in China and the Margin of Appreciation Doctrine: A Legal Analysis of the Crackdown on the Falun Gong and Other 'Evil Cults,'" *Journal of Church and State*, Spring 2005.

Cathy Lynn
Grossman   "'Code' and the Sacred Feminine: Has Religion Denied Women Their Due?" *USA Today*, May 24, 2006.

Helen Hardacre "From Salvation to Spirituality: Popular Religious Movements in Modern Japan," *Journal of Asian Studies*, February 2006.

Dennis Harvey "The People's Temple," *Variety*, May 16–22, 2005.

Sterling Haynes "How Illness Saved a Boy and Set Him Free," *Medical Post*, November 1, 2005.

Bill Hewitt and Maureen Harrington "Was the Family Doing God's Work—or Unspeakable Harm?" *People*, July 18, 2005.

Massimo Introvigne "The Future of New Religions," *Futures*, November 2004.

Philip Jenkins "Cult Classics," *Atlantic Monthly*, April 2006.

Judy Keen "Maharishi Meets the Bible Belt: But Not Everyone in Kansas Town Blissful over Plans to Create 'World Capital of Peace,'" *USA Today*, May 23, 2006.

Don Lattin "Global Cult," *Investigative Reporters and Editors (IRE) Journal*, September/October 2005.

Oleg Liakhovich "Beslan Mothers Split over Resurrection Cult," *Moscow News*, October 5–11, 2005.

NEA Today "Clear Your Mind," May 2006.

Paul J. Olson "The Public Perception of 'Cults' and 'New Religious Movements,'" *Journal for the Scientific Study of Religion*, March 2006.

Roger E. Olson "Pentecostalism's Dark Side," *Christian Century*, March 7, 2006.

Graeme Paton "Official Backing for the Brethren," *Times Educational Supplement*, August 12, 2005.

Leah Paulos "Family Betrayal," *Seventeen*, April 2006.

Susan Raine "Reconceptualising the Human Body: Heaven's Gate and the Quest for Divine Transformation," *Religion*, April 2005.

Janet Reitman "Inside Scientology," *Rolling Stone*, March 9, 2006.

James T. Richardson and Masssimo Introvigne "'Brainwashing' Theories in European Parliamentary and Administrative Reports on 'Cults' and 'Sects,'" *Journal for the Scientific Study of Religion*, June 2001.

Thomas Robbins "Combating 'Cults' and 'Brainwashing' in the United States and Western Europe: A Comment on Richardson and Introvigne's Report," *Journal for the Scientific Study of Religion*, June 2001.

Larry Rohter	"At Cult's Enclave in Chile, Guns and Intelligence Files," *New York Times (Late Edition, East Coast)*, June 17, 2005.
Larry Rohter	"Guru of Sadism, Safely in Jail, Leaves Cult to Fend for Itself," *New York Times (Late Edition, East Coast)*, May 16, 2005.
Larry Rohter	"World Briefing Americas: Chile: Cult Leader Gets 20 Years," *New York Times (Late Edition, East Coast)*, May 25, 2006.
Abdurrahman Wahid	"Right Islam vs. Wrong Islam," *Wall Street Journal (Eastern Edition)*, December 30, 2005.
Peter Wilkinson	"The Life and Death of the Chosen One," *Rolling Stone*, June 30–July 14, 2005.
Jim Winkates	"Suicide Terrorism: Martyrdom for Organizational Objectives," *Journal of Third World Studies*, Spring 2006.
Karl Zinsmeister	"Faithful Community Life," *American Enterprise*, May 2006.

Web Sites

Doomsday, Destructive Religious Cults (www.religioustoler ance.org/destruct.htm). Maintained by Canadian Bruce A. Robinson's organization Ontario Consultants on Religious Tolerance, this division of a comprehensive archive of essays on religion, spirituality, and ethics defines and analyzes (among tens of thousands of new religious groups worldwide) those groups that are proven or are considered potentially dangerous.

International Cultic Studies Association (www.csj.org). This comprehensive, recommended site offers articles, discussion forums, an e-newsletter, and updated information on hundreds of cultic groups and movements. The site presents both positive and negative opinions and encourages inquiry aimed at making independent and informed judgments about whether a specific listed group—mainstream or nonmainstream, controversial or noncontroversial—is harmful or benign.

Index